Written on the Knee

Written on the Knee

A Diary from the Greek-Italian Front of WWII

Diary by Dr. Theodore Electris

TRANSLATED WITH COMMENTARY
by HELEN ELECTRIE LINDSAY

SCARLETTA PRESS

MINNEAPOLIS

SCARLETTA PRESS

10 South Fifth Street, Suite 1105, Minneapolis, MN 55402, USA

Visit our website at www.scarlettapress.com

Library of Congress Cataloging-in-Publication Data

Electris, Theodore.

   Written on the knee : a diary from the Greek-Italian front of WWII / diary by Theodore Electris ; translated with commentary by Helen Electrie Lindsay.—1st ed.

      p.   cm.

   ISBN 13: 978-0-9798249-3-7 (pbk.)
   ISBN 10: 0-9798249-3-1

1. Electris, Theodore—Diaries. 2. World War, 1939–1945—Medical care—Greece. 3. Greece. Stratos—Medical personnel—Diaries. 4. World War, 1939–1945—Campaigns—Albania. 5. World War, 1939–1945—Personal narratives, Greek. 6. Physicians—Greece—Diaries. I. Lindsay, Helen Electrie. II. Title.

   D807.G8E44 2008
   940.54'75495092—dc22
   [B]

                                                                           2008034296

Book design by Mighty Media Inc., Minneapolis, MN
Cover: Anders Hanson   Interior: Chris Long

First edition

10 9 8 7 6 5 4 3 2 1

Printed in Canada

Στην αγαπημένη μου
γυναικούλα Χρυσούλα

To my beloved little wife, Chrysoula

... I have recorded events as they occurred and action as it was taken. Later on, these can be judged in the glare of consequences; and finally, when our lives have faded, history will pronounce its cool, detached and shadowy verdict.

SIR WINSTON CHURCHILL

ΓΛΥΚΥ Δ΄ ΑΠΕΙΡΟΙΣΙ ΠΟΛΕΜΟΣ

War is sweet to those who never experienced it.

PINDAR

Contents

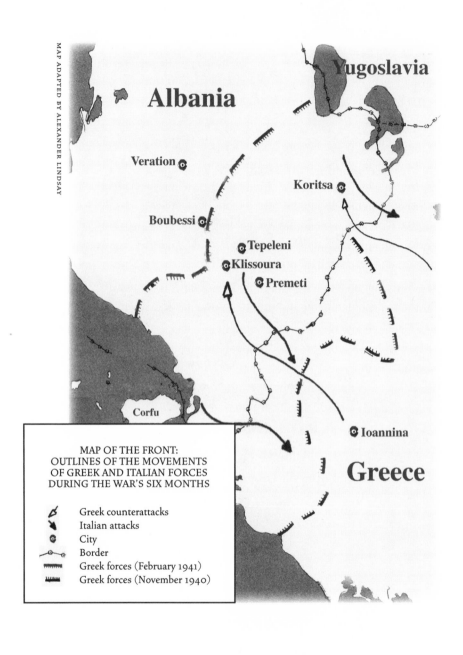

Yugoslavia

Albania

Veration

Koritsa

Boubessi

Tepeleni
Klissoura
Premeti

Corfu

Ioannina

Greece

MAP OF THE FRONT:
OUTLINES OF THE MOVEMENTS
OF GREEK AND ITALIAN FORCES
DURING THE WAR'S SIX MONTHS

Greek counterattacks
Italian attacks
City
Border
Greek forces (February 1941)
Greek forces (November 1940)

Introduction

I once wrote somewhere that history ought to consist of the anecdotes of the little people who get caught up in it. My own feeling for history derives from hearing my parents' reminiscences and reflections about the Second World War, usually at the dinner table. They would often mention people who had been killed, or places that had been destroyed, and I always had the feeling that they were quite surprised to be still living themselves. My mother was a signals officer directing submarines in the Indian Ocean, and my father was initially in North Africa, and then in the hideous battles in Italy on the Gothic Line. One of my grandfathers was horribly injured in the First World War, and finally committed suicide. I had a grandmother who lost her first fiancé in 1915. It is hard to imagine what would have happened to all these little people if history had not intervened in their lives.

As a list of dates and of the exploits of great generals and politicians, history is almost meaningless except as a useful chronology. This book, however, exactly fits my prescription, being the diary of a doctor from Thessaloniki who found himself being sent to the Albanian Front in 1940. This campaign is little remembered outside Greece. The Italians don't like to recall that they started on the wrong side, and Britain was almost completely preoccupied with its own war against Germany, although troops from the empire were eventually sent in numbers too small and too late. Greece was the last remaining British ally.

In Greece the campaign is very much remembered and celebrated, and is a focus of national pride. Mussolini had demanded that Italian troops should be allowed to enter and occupy Greece "for reasons of security," and General Metaxas, the prime minister of Greece, and effectively its military dictator, had refused outright. Modern Greeks tend to be uncharitable to Metaxas' memory, and commemorate "Ochi" day ("No" day) as if it were all of Greece which had refused, rather than one proud and sick old man. Greece certainly stood behind him, however, and Greek soldiers roundly defeated the Italian armies in a series of engagements, driving them back into Albania. Readers of this diary will discover how appalling the conditions were, and in parenthesis I would recommend Mario Cervi's *Hollow Legions* as a superb account of the same campaign from an Italian perspective.

Hitler was forced to invade Greece through Bulgaria in order to save Mussolini from ignominy. This caused a delay to the invasion of Russia, and so the hitherto victorious German invaders perished in the bitter winter, just as Napoleon's armies had before them. It is certainly arguable that in resisting the Italians so successfully, the Greek soldiers changed the course of history, and laid the foundations for the ultimate Allied victory.

Dr. Electris' diary is a very telling account of what it is like to be a soldier, even though, as a doctor, he would not have had to bear arms in action. He tells of the daily search for food and warmth, the confusion, the constant moving from one place to another without ever really knowing why, the aching bones and exhaustion, the rivalries that spring up and just as quickly melt away, the often heartwarming encounters with civilians in remote places, the near-misses and shocking moments of violence, the impossibility of coping without proper medical supplies, the relishing of a rare cigarette, the horror of being lost and separated from your unit in the midst of a wilderness, the floundering of stretcher-bearers in mud, the deaths of pack animals and a beloved horse, and the sheer waste of all that gets abandoned in retreat.

More importantly, the diary tells of what kept this particular soldier going: love for a wife and the longing to be reunited with her, concern for a sister and for the family cat, and the determination to be an effective doctor in the face of impossible difficulties. Dr. Electris lives for the letters from his wife, Chrysoula, and his family. Indeed the diary reads as if it were written specifically for Chrysoula, with the intention that she should read it when and if he comes home. They had been married only a few months before mobilisation, and they were both full of the passion and sweetness of newlyweds. At the last, with the Greek army breaking apart, all he can think of is how to get home. He somehow manages to get back to Thessaloniki despite having nothing at all in his possession. This is what in fact every Greek soldier had to do after the war was lost, and the countryside must have been crawling with thousands of Odysseuses, all improvising their impossible way back to their particular Ithaca.

The diary ends happily with the doctor and Chrysoula reunited, but of course the sense of closure is a false one. For Dr. Electris there followed an immense labour as he coped with sick and starving Greeks for the rest of the war, and then again of course during the civil war that began immediately afterwards. One wonders what his diaries of these periods might have been like. It is perhaps enough that he left us with this small gem, written artlessly, and without any thought that it might be of interest to posterity. In these pages the warm heart of a dead man beats again, his passions are re-lived, his pleasures, hardships, and irritations unfold for us as if they were in the present. Such is the immediacy of the writing that it is not at all hard for us to feel that we know the doctor, and share his experiences. He was a little person, to be sure, but like so many other worthy people of his generation, he was someone who put his shoulder to the wheel of history, and made a difference. These are his stories, revealing that a soldier's heroism resides not so much in his flashes of glory, but in endurance sustained by hope.

LOUIS de BERNIÈRES
MARCH 2008

Prologue

This wartime diary, the centerpiece of *Written on the Knee*, has no pretensions to literary greatness. It does recount a few valorous deeds, but mostly it records many ordinary, non-heroic human acts, feelings and thoughts of one man, a medic, caught in the crumbling chaos of an anguishing expedition to defend his country against unjust Axis aggression. Written during Italy's invasion of Greece in World War II, this humble journal tells of the passion, desire and pathos of a common citizen in his resolute struggle to survive. In the face of great adversity, Dr. Theodore Electris affirms his longing for the most basic, yet to him chimerical, happiness in life: the freedom to follow his calling as a physician, with his beloved wife at his side and surrounded by the people who love him in his home, his "nest."

This diary is also a testimony to the transforming and saving power of love and commitment to one's spouse, family and friends. The diarist is concerned for the well-being of each member of his family even from the battlefront. The loved ones at home support him by sending care packages and letters. He survives in order to return to his beloved wife, to whom he had been married for only three months prior to leaving for the front. His wife, my mother, a delicate and pampered young person, a novice in life, emerges as a strong and capable woman.

World War II changed the life of my family dramatically—and tragically. This war was the fourth in a series of major disruptions that my family endured, following World War I, the Russian Revolution and the Asia Minor Destruction.[1] It was also the cause of the disease that led to my father's death. In addition, the hasty and chaotic retreat during the German invasion denied him recognition of his military service.[2]

I bring this diary to light especially for my children and my brother's children, and the relatives, friends and patients who knew and loved my father and mother. I feel that by publishing it I am fulfilling the wishes of my father, who believed in the lasting power of the written word and wanted to publish it but was prevented, by circumstances after the war, from doing so.

My father was well versed in European history and politics. He knew that an ordinary citizen is often a pawn in the hands of the Great Powers, pushed about by the currents of history. Nevertheless, he was courageous and optimistic, and up to the last moment of his life he dared to believe, even in the face of absurdities and disappointments, that the words and deeds of every man are not in vain but have a special place and significance in human existence and in the universe.

For this reason he hoped that his participation in the struggle on the Greek-Italian front, as well as his work in post-WWII Thessaloniki, contributed, even if only in a minute way, to the freedom and the well-being of his country and the happiness of his children.

HELEN ELECTRIE LINDSAY

---

1   After fighting alongside the Allies during World War I, the Greeks gained the territory of Western Thrace and more of the Aegean Islands. But in 1919 they tried to reclaim the Greek-inhabited territory of Smyrna, and even attempted to grab Istanbul. They campaigned in Asia Minor with initial success, but Kemal Ataturk fought the Greeks and drove them out of Smyrna. His army slaughtered Smyrna's Greek population and the surrounding Hellenic towns and villages, burning them down. This genocide is referred to as the Asia Minor Destruction. The treaty that followed provided for an "Exchange of Populations." Greece received almost 1.5 million Greek refugees (who left everything behind), increasing its population by twenty-five percent, while Turkey received four hundred thousand Turks. This ended a two-thousand-year-old presence of Hellenic civilization in Asia Minor.

2   In the entry for April 14, Dr. Electris mentioned that he was anticipating receiving a medal for exceptional service with his unit.

Historical Context:

The State of Europe in 1940

MAP ADAPTED BY ALEXANDER LINDSAY

By October 1940, Europe was being overtaken bit by bit by the forces of the Axis in the west and by Russia in the east. Germany occupied the Rhineland (taken in 1936), Austria (1938), the Czech Sudetenland (October 1938), and dismembered Czechoslovakia (March 1939). It also occupied Bohemia and Moravia. The attack on Prague began to change the policy of "appeasement" followed by British Prime Minister Neville Chamberlain. The new strategy was to construct an Eastern European alliance against Germany. At the same time, Hitler's move against Prague emboldened Mussolini, who forcibly annexed Albania. Concerned with the German and Italian moves, the French and the British offered a guarantee to Greece to defend it against aggression. On May 23, 1939, the Rome-Berlin axis became a "Steel Pact."[3]

Germany and Russia had partitioned Poland in September 1939. Russia attacked Finland in the period of 1939–40. By June 1940 Norway, Belgium, Denmark and France had fallen under Hitler's control and Stalinist Russia controlled the Baltic states. On the 10th of July that year, Hitler began the bombing of Britain. In September 1940, Axis powers Germany, Italy and Japan signed the Tripartite Pact; Hungary and Romania joined the Axis by the end of the year.

The Battle of Britain in summer and autumn of 1940 persuaded Hitler to change course; abandoning attempts at direct domination, he decided instead to pursue a "peripheral strategy" aimed at cutting off the British Empire from its allies and colonies. He was also getting increasingly annoyed with Stalin's grab and Sovietization of Eastern European lands.[4] He hoped that either the Soviets would join the Axis or Germany would take over the Soviet Union, thus forcing Britain to face Hitler as the sole master of the continent. By July 1940 "... he summed up his credo: 'Russia is the factor by which England sets the greatest store.... If Russia is beaten, England's last hope is gone.'"[5] As early as the summer of 1940, Hitler began to consider the possibility of invading Russia.

---

3   Lukacs, pp. 36–47.
4   Lukacs, p. 103.
5   Sulzberger, p. 55.

In the Balkans, however, Hitler did not wish to disturb the balance of power, because he wanted neither the British nor the Russians to be drawn into that area. Germany was extracting essential raw materials from the Balkan countries, including pyrites, iron, chrome, nickel ore, manganese, wheat, and most important, oil, which was taken from the Ploesti oil fields in Romania. Oil shipments to Germany from the United States and Venezuela had stopped by 1939, and by 1940 most of Germany's oil was imported from Romania and Russia. By 1941 Romania was the only European country that could provide the Nazis with oil. Through deceit, economic and diplomatic pressures, and outright bullying, Hitler maintained an artificial calm and stability on the Balkan peninsula in order to ensure an uninterrupted source of critical supplies to areas where he needed them.

Among these Balkan countries, however, Greece was different. With its island archipelago it could play an important role in upsetting Hitler's "peripheral strategy." Most threatening, Greece could provide the British with bases for their bombers. Greece and its island of Crete provided the furthest point in southern Europe from which the British planes (of that technological period) could reach and destroy the Ploesti oil fields.

Greece was then governed by Ioannis Metaxas, a dictator who cast a sympathetic eye towards the governments of Germany and Italy. Trade was a major factor in the relationship between Greece and the Axis, since Germany was absorbing most of Greece's exports. On the other hand, Metaxas realized that Greece's political fortunes were closely connected to Great Britain; historically, the Greek people felt greater kinship with the British than with the Germans. Greece, like Britain, was a naval power. Most important, though, Metaxas was beginning to be weary of the pressure he felt from Mussolini's expansionism. Being a pragmatist, he walked a very delicate line, attempting to keep Greece neutral and, at the same time, not provoke an invasion by the Axis forces.

Meanwhile, Mussolini was concerned that he was being excluded from the Axis actions and became upset that Hitler did not inform him of major operations anywhere. He decided to pay Hitler back with a "fait accompli" by invading Greece. On August 15, 1940 (a religious holiday in Greece), he provoked the Greeks by torpedoing the Greek cruiser *Helle* in the harbor of the island of Tinos. On October 28, 1940, at 2:30 A.M., the Italian embassador to Greece visited Metaxas' house and demanded an immediate surrender of Greece to Italy. The Greek dictator, wearing his nightclothes, delivered his famous response: "Ochi!" ("No!"). Greece was engulfed in WWII.

Some historians argue that Hitler approved an assault on Greece by Italy and advised Mussolini to carry out a blitzkrieg-style operation on Crete, thus enabling the Axis forces to dominate the eastern Mediterranean and isolate Britain from its Middle East allies. Had Mussolini followed Hitler's suggestions and been successful, Hitler would have faced no problems in the Balkans. His planned invasion of Russia would have left the rear relatively undisturbed. However, Mussolini's fiasco threatened the larger Axis plan and made the German diversion through the Balkans a necessity.

The Greek-Italian war is a very brief chapter in the history of WWII. It lasted only six months—from October 1940 to April 1941, when the Germans invaded the Balkans and overran Greece. The Greeks defeated the Italians and forced them back into Albania. Hitler, frustrated with the Italian defeat, worried that instead of isolating the British in the Eastern Mediterranean, he was drawing them into Greece. He feared the British would establish their bases in Crete and in Thessaloniki. The Italian blunder made it necessary for Hitler to begin planning the invasion of Greece, as early as November 1940. Hitler's #20 confidential directive was issued on December 13, 1940: the attack against Greece, code name "Operation Marita."[6]

By November 11, 1940, after a meeting with the Russian Foreign Minister Vyacheslav Molotov, Hitler decided that Russia was demanding too much for continued forbearance within the framework of the Alliance. So he chose to invade Russia with Operation Barbarossa, issued with directive #21 on December 18, 1940.[7] The

---

6   *Abridged History*, p. 168.
7   Ibid, p. 169.

invasion of Greece therefore became doubly important: first, to protect the Ploesti oil fields from the British; and second, to secure the German right flank while they were invading Russia.

Subsequently, through his blitzkrieg strategies, Hitler conquered the Balkans and Greece. Greece's last outpost, Crete, fell in the first-ever German air-assault in June of 1941 in Operation Mercury, despite being bravely defended by British and Greek forces.

...

The diary of Dr. Electris begins at the start of the Greek-Italian war and ends with the German invasion of Greece.

On October 28, 1940, my father, Dr. Theodore (Phaedia[8]) Electris, and thousands of other Greek civilians were mobilized and ordered to proceed to the Western Front to support the Greek army, which was trying to stop the advancing Italian armies.

He had to leave behind his medical practice and—closest to his heart—his beloved bride of three months. The front destination was the Greek-Albanian border, almost 250 miles from his home city Thessaloniki, on a terrain of nearly impassable rugged mountains. What follows are excerpts from his almost daily entries in the diary he kept (from the day he left to the day that he returned home), supplemented by letters that he wrote to my mother as well as some of her letters to him.

My father was part of the B Division of the Greek army under General Tsipouras and later under General Demaratos. All through November their unit advanced through the very rugged mountains and torrential rivers of northwestern Greece, staying off the main roads for better cover. They withstood extremely harsh weather, foraging and scavenging for food. In the beginning of December they crossed into Albania, pursuing the retreating Italians. Their first camp location was near Kakosi [Kakos][9], where they stayed for about a month. As the Italians retreated they moved deeper into Al-

---

8   "Phaedia" is the familiar form of "Theodore" in Russian. Dr. Electris was a
    Pontic Greek raised in Russia (currently Georgia).

9   Names used in brackets are the modern Albanian and Greek names, as
    opposed to Greek names used in the diary.

bania. The continuous bombing forced them to keep moving camp sites. Their location was on the mountains to the west of the city of Sorovod [Corovode].

The Greek army's goals were to capture Klissoura [Kelcyre], Tepeleni [Tepelene] and Veration [Berat]. Along the front line that was established west of Corovode to Kelcyre, some of the fiercest battles were fought in order to capture certain heights[10] or mountain peaks.

That front line was held until April 14, 1941. On that day the Greek army was ordered to fall back quickly to the Greek borders without being defeated. That retreat was imperative because the German army invaded Greece from the northeast and the soldiers at the Albanian front were in danger of being caught between the Germans and the Italians. The events that followed—the capitulation of the Greeks to the Germans, the disbanding of the Greek army—were chaotic. By the beginning of May my father found his way home.

The diary begins on the day he departed for the front.

---

10 Each mountain height was labeled and identified with a number, sometimes referenced in the diary.

Ἀρ. Ε.Π 681/410

ΜΟΝΑΣ ΧΙ ΣΥΝ/ΜΑ ΠΥΡ/ΚΟΥ

ΦΥΛΛΟΝ
ΑΤΟΜΙΚΗΣ ΠΡΟΣΚΛΗΣΕΩΣ

Δυνάμει τοῦ Νόμου 4324 καί κατόπιν Διαταγῆς τοῦ Ὑπουργείου Στρατιωτικῶν

ΚΑΛΟΓΜΕΝ

Τὸν Ἔφεδρον Στρατιώτην Ἠλέμτρην Θεόδωρον τοῦ Σταύρου

ἐκ Θεσλνίμης τῆς Ἐπαρχίας Θεσλνίμης

κλάσεως 1927. Α.Σ.Μ. 9407 Ἀριθ. Γ.Ε.Ε. Ἀριθ. Μ.Ε.Ε.

κάτοικον Θεσλνίμης Διεύθυνσις κατοικίας Ἀλατίνη

Συνοικία Δημοσιογράφων (Υ. δ. γ.)

ὅπως παρουσιασθῇ ἐντὸς ὡρῶν εἰς (Μονάς, τόπος) τὴν 7ην Ἀπριλίου 1940

καὶ ὥραν 7.30 π.μ. εἰς ΧΙ. Σύνταγμα Πυρικοῦ.

Ὁ μὴ συμμορφούμενος Ἔφεδρος, κηρυσσόμενος ἀνυπότακτος, τιμωρεῖται ὑπὸ τοῦ Στρατοδικείου συμφώ-
νως τῷ Νόμῳ μὲ φυλάκισιν μέχρι πέντε (5) ἐτῶν καὶ μὲ πρόστιμον ἀπὸ 5000 μέχρι 500.000 Δραχμῶν.

Αἱ κατὰ τόπους Ἀστυνομικαὶ Ἀρχαὶ ὑποχρεοῦνται νὰ διευκολύνωσι τὸν ἔφεδρον διὰ τὴν ταχυτέραν
ἀναχώρησίν του τῇ ἐπιδείξει τοῦ παρόντος.

Ἐπεδόθη

Τὴν 7 Μαρτίου 1940

καὶ ὥραν 2930

Ὁ Ἐπιδούς

Ἐν Θεσλνίμῃ τῇ 26 Μαρτίου 1940

Ὁ Διοικητής

*Mobilization notice, dated April 7, 1940, ordering Dr. Theodore Electris to report
to artillery unit XI as a reservist.*

Diary

"Mobilization, mobilization ... we are being mobilized ..."

PHOTO BY DR. THEODORE ELECTRIS

Our unit.

November 1, 1940

Mobilization, mobilization ... we are being mobilized ...

Around 2:00 P.M. we started from camp, taking the side roads, walking towards the Harmanakion [Alexandria][11] station. We arrived there around 4:00 P.M. Halfway there were two air raids; we scattered and took cover in the surrounding hills.

All morning long, before we departed, I waited for my sweet wife, so I could say goodbye; I was worried that she might have encountered an air raid as well. She finally came just as we were pulling out. My sweetheart, my love, why should she have to suffer so much, only because I love her?! She loves me too and I feel it. For her love I can withstand anything.

Thumbnail map indicates Dr. Electris' position on the date to which the diary refers.

Soon we will board trains that will take us to Sorovich [Amynteo].

All along during our move I worried about her return to the house. This "worry" thing is a newly developed feeling and is gripping us all with its claws; it's worse than fear itself.

With these thoughts and emotions I look for a phone and call her. My heart opens to her sweet voice like the flowers do in the morning sun; it caresses my ears and gives me so much courage! Now I know she is well, but in her voice I detect a tremble, a concealed concern. Perhaps she encountered an air raid on her way back, perhaps it's her worry for me. I will forever love her and want her, no matter how far away I am from her.

It's dark now and unfortunately we are ordered to go back to the station in the Free Zone[12] in order to board the trains for Sorovich ... and so, here I am again following on horseback, wearing the typical helmet of a sublieutenant of our squadron.

We arrived at the station around 11:00 P.M. and did not leave until 5:00 A.M. To start with, all officers, including our commander, are boarded on a freight train. I use my bags for pillows. Later,

---

11   Cities in brackets are the modern names, not the ones used in the diary.
12   The port area.

though, we are upgraded to an excursion train. There I meet up with another reservist colleague, Sites. He is an old classmate from medical school. I hope that we'll be good *parea*[13] for each other. The colonel of our unit, who is on the train as well, is a very nice and well-educated man.

November 2, 1940

I cannot shut my eyes, even for a moment. It is morning and we are still talking about the destruction that the Italians will bring upon Thessaloniki. This "worry" thing attacks again ... it comes in waves, forcing itself on every bit of my existence ...

Now we are pulling into Gidas; here my colleague and I buy four small bottles of cognac and two cans of sardines for sixty drachmas.

I regret that I haven't brought my rainwear, my gloves, my camera and other things ... but we left in such a rush that I did not even have time to say goodbye to my sweet wife.

It is 9:30 A.M. and we just passed Platy. We learn that Thessaloniki was bombed. We have left there and so we are not in as much danger as our houses, our nests, our loves, our lives ... This "worry" gets hold of me again—I wonder, will we unlearn this feeling after the war is over, or will we forever carry the germ of its neurosis?

This last train ride brings us into Sorovich around 5:00 P.M.; here we camp and eat. We are supposed to move again at midnight.

November 3, 1940

The weather so far had been good, but the moment we started off again, it began to rain. Alas, we had a walk of at least 20 km[14] ahead of us. My colleague, having no horse, left for our destination by car, but I was not so fortunate. My hostler, by mistake, had saddled my

---

13   The Greek word *parea* means more than "buddies"—almost brothers.
14   12.4 miles; 1 kilometer equals approximately 0.62 mile.

PHOTO: GEO MAGAZINE, OCTOBER 18, 2001

Aerial view of the village of Sklethron.

horse with an old saddle, and as the horse moved, it rubbed roughly against my inner thigh. In addition, the stirrups were set too high and my knees were hurting. I did not want to stop for adjustments for fear of getting out of line. All of that would not have bothered me had it not been raining cataclysmically, soaking us to the bone. I rode for 10 km and then walked the rest in that rain and mud and the mountain winds of the province of Florina.

Finally, at 7:00 the next morning, we arrived in the town of Sklethron. Our first priority was to make sure our poor soldiers had the best possible camping arrangements. After that, I looked for the house that my colleague was staying in. There I washed my feet, changed to the warmest clothes I had and asked the landlady's daughters to dry my clothes. I had some hot lamb soup with rice and covered myself with several blankets. At 1:00 P.M. I ate again, got dressed and went outside.

Sklethron is a nice village, but damp. For a while it has been sunny and we are enjoying nature. I'm sorry that I don't have my camera. We were supposed to go to Argos, but now we are changing directions.

November 4, 1940

Yesterday at 6:00 P.M. we started marching westward towards Kaylaria [Ptolemais]. Before we left I went to the post office and mailed a letter to my sweet wife, who most probably is worried about me.

We arrived in the town of Perdikkas, which is in the province of Ptolemais, after a 45 km walk. It was around 4:40 A.M.

We stayed with Mr. Prodromos Iakovides. He is also known as Bosos Agas. We were able to sleep until 12:30 P.M., and when we woke up we lunched on warm village bread, fresh butter, salty cheese and warm tea. (I had five cups!) Then I did the patient rounds while my nurses and hostler took care of all of our supplies and my horse.

At 5:00 P.M. we'll again start the walk towards Ptolemais, and from there we'll go to Kozani. Happily, I'll be on horseback.

November 5, 1940

Yesterday I had too many patients and little time for writing. Our daily march continued and we walked 35 km. We started at 7:00 P.M. and arrived in the village of Kila around 4:00 A.M. The weather was pleasant and I decided to walk.

In Kila all the officers stayed in a hay barn. We made beds with hay and slept with all our clothes on. When we awoke around 9:00 A.M. it was very cold. I felt a lot better after I went to the restaurant and had a full breakfast of eggs, sausage and hot tea. It looks as if today we will have a shorter walk. We will camp 5 km outside Kozani.

This "worry" thing is clawing at me again ... I wonder how my sweet wife is. At least, my mother and all others are not in Thessaloniki, so I don't have to worry about them too ... My sweet Chrysoula, most probably she is not eating or sleeping well. How I wish I could be close to her to console her and hug and kiss her. If she were to see me now, she would not recognize me. I look so bad ... I haven't shaved since we started off from Thessaloniki; perhaps I'll grow a beard. Now I'm going to look for some water and try to give my feet a warm bath.

November 6, 1940

We started early and 30 km later arrived in the village of Mesopotamos. It is deserted now and we were assigned to various houses. My colleague and I were assigned to the same house. We slept on the floor. Somewhere close by, guns were being fired. Today we are well rested and I shaved. We ate together with our nurses and I wrote a letter to my sweet wife. We'll start marching again around 5:00 P.M.

November 7, 1940

We walked for a very long time and the only reprieve was that the trip was pleasant. The moon rose over the small villages, making them magically picturesque. I had the bizarre sensation that I was living in a dream, that reality was elsewhere and I would wake up in it, just around the corner—but that corner was getting farther and farther away from me.

We walked in small units so we would not be a target for enemy planes.

I forgot to write the names of the officers of our units. Our colonel and leader is Mr. Drungas; the other officers are Captain Baltas, Lieutenants Christopoulos and Anagnostou and Sublieutenants Katzurakis, Makrides, Evnouhides, Perperis, Veziroglou and Lefkopulos, and Adjutant Velides.

After walking 29 km we arrived in the village of Rodia. We were informed that enemy planes were performing reconnaissance missions from great heights. Perhaps they had been informed that our army was going to go through here. For better protection the soldiers and the animals had to stay in the forest. Meanwhile, my colleague Sites, who always manages to find things we need, discovered two divans and a fireplace in a cafe. We drank tea, covered up (I actually found a duvet and a sheet), and went to sleep. I would never have imagined that I could ever sleep with such pleasure on such a mattress! I am amazed how our bodies can withstand these kinds of hardships.

Finding something decent to eat is another business. I'm actually the arrogant gourmand who fell from the grace of the gods. From a great lover of food—who would even critique the grains of salt in each meal I ate—I have been reduced to a scavenger. One should not be too cocky and hypercritical about anything, even food.

Well, if I look at things from a different perspective, perhaps this deprivation will turn me into a better person; perhaps I'll learn how to cook better. I'm sure that after this expedition I will even be able to make rocks taste good ...

In any case, our nurse found us some eggs, and Sites found some olives and pickled cabbage and a quince (which we didn't get to eat because someone stole it). For lunch we cooked two roosters; we saved our dry foods for tougher times. Happily, my colleague has money and our supplies never end.

November 8, 1940

After eating some chicken soup we were revived and ready for the next march, which was almost continuous. We started about 7:00 P.M. last evening and ended around 10:00 A.M. today, with only a short stop at the village of Megara.

I will never forget last night's odyssey. It was a 15-hour torturous march in a constant sprinkle on steep mountainsides and at very high altitude; the experience transcended war ... The continuous lines of lights winding up the mountain paths, against the backdrop of the deep, dark ravines, were wildly graphic, but awesome and overwhelming. The whole sight had an aura of a religious pilgrimage and it reminded me of a torchlight procession of Buddhist monks that I had read about.

I wish I knew how to use this pen to better describe this war. I wish I could transfer onto paper the tremendous and exhaustive effort made to traverse these almost impassable mountains and cross these abysmal ravines ... Maybe it's just as well that I'm not so good with the pen, because if I were successful in describing the energy spent and transferring it to paper, this paper might ignite ...

Anyway, after a 50 km march we finally arrived outside the village of Dotsiko, where we camped.

Three trucks with Italian prisoners of war passed by. The prisoners were so young, just children!

We were supposed to stop 10 km from our present camp, but now the plans are to follow the Italians, who are retreating.

Today I do not plan to write a letter to my wife because I have no way of sending it to her.

November 10, 1940

The past two days I camped with the 8th Infantry Unit. I took care of a wounded man—John Tsigaros; then I gave him my home address and asked him to look for my wife. The 8th element had to start marching again in the morning despite the cataclysmic rain. About 7:00 A.M. I packed my patient's things and put him on a horse. I took him to the transfer station at Dotsiko and then I continued on the way to Samarina, 15 km away.

This impossible and nearly impassable pass we had to cross is beyond imagination. Dead horses and guns were scattered everywhere. We ascended and ascended to incredible heights. It was snowing and storming and I thought that we were finished. Fortunately I had a bottle of cognac from which I took a few sips from time to time. I also shared it with the three soldiers who accompanied me. I was trying to hurry up so I was ahead of the group. As we climbed higher and higher my feet kept freezing, so I got off my horse and walked. On the way I met someone who was a bus inspector in Thessaloniki. He was hungry and thirsty, and I shared my bread and brandy with him.

Despite the cold weather I could not stop admiring that incredible landscape. The mountains were majestic and the pine trees so immense that three men together would have had a hard time putting their arms around their trunks. After crossing a river we finally arrived to Samarina. It was an impressive village. In the village square there were huge spruce and pine trees. It was prettier than a Swiss village.

I looked for the house where the officers were settled, brought all my things, took all my clothes off and started drying them, but

PHOTO: GEO MAGAZINE, MARCH 1, 2003

The village of Samarina.

all of a sudden I realized the fireplace chimney had caught fire and the house was burning. I had a hard time waking up the officers because they were sleeping so deeply. Another doctor and I moved all our medical supplies and some blankets to the school. Subsequently all other officers settled there. I forgot to say that when I first entered the village I found a ring, which I stuck deep inside my jacket pocket as a memento from the war.

I don't know where they are taking us. Perhaps we will try to go back, because it appears that the front is really settled and many Italians have been captured.

In the morning all the officers packed heavy blankets inside their tents to be prepared for any colder weather ahead. If only our feet could be dry; when they are dry, all problems are forgotten.

No one can imagine how people act in this cold weather. Everyone tried to take a blanket or some piece of warm clothing as booty. I even took a small fur to wear underneath my sweater. This village was completely plundered by our army; unfortunately it had been plundered previously by the Italians. The traitors who showed the Italians the path to the Greek lands were from this village. The result was that they advanced 50 km onto Greek soil. Now both the Italians and the villagers paid for their aggression. Ninety-five percent of the village is deserted. In the house where I am now, I am heating some water in the fireplace to wash my feet.

November 11, 1940

Yesterday at about 3:30 P.M. some Greek and English bomber planes dropped sacks of *kouramanes*[15] because supplying us on this impassable road would otherwise have been impossible. There was also an accident where one of the soldiers was hit by one of the sacks and suffered a slight concussion.

The officers and the doctors ate together and slept in the same rooms, though we did not have enough covers and got cold. Somehow some soldiers found flour and oil and made fried bread. It was a real treat!

---

15   Round loaves of wheat bread.

After I checked my medical supplies, I reserved the afternoon for patient rounds. Meanwhile the sirens were sounding because an enemy plane was spotted.

At this moment it is noon and anti-aircraft guns are being fired from our camp in Samarina, where many other regiments are camping. Half an hour ago I wrote two notes to my mother and to my wife and gave them to a soldier who was going to a hospital in Kozani. I am going to the command center to find out what is happening.

November 12, 1940

Yesterday at noon we ate well: bean soup and fried veal livers! Around 3:00 I did patient rounds and asked my assistant to wash some of my underclothes.

Meanwhile there was another air raid. When the sun goes down it gets chilly. After all, Samarina is at an altitude of 1,500 m. In the evening another house burned down. Last night I kept warmer and this morning I got up later. I have patient rounds in the morning. So far we are alright. Perhaps one can imagine that we are vacationing in such altitude. I wrote a letter to my wife, which I'll try to send with another wounded soldier. For lunch we'll have chicken soup.

> *Nov. 12, 1940*
> *My dearest Phaedia,*
>
> *After 12 days of agony I finally received from you a single card, and it had no date ... You write me that you are well: "We are all well" ... Please, write and tell me if you would like me to send you money or whatever else you need. I'm knitting for you a warm woolen long sleeve sweater. It is the one that I started for you that was supposed to be sleeveless. I will send it to you at the address of this letter. Do not worry about the bombing raids here. I'm not afraid and I have a lot of courage. Please, only take care of yourself and please, write to me every day: I can die just from agony, just waiting to get a letter from you. Tell me if I could come and meet you somewhere.*

I will send your news to your mother and sisters in Athens.
Your father here is very well.
Greetings from everyone.
Kisses,
Chrysoula

November 13, 1940

The day passed uneventfully. Last night Colonel Nikas and Dr. Kastanoudakis joined our group. Perhaps we will stay here for a while or perhaps we will move towards Konitsa, where it would be easier to supply us because the roads are better.

November 14, 1940

At about 2:00 P.M. we got ready for departure. It is now 11:15 and we are in Epirus, where we are waiting for our unit, which has been broken up. We passed ravines and valleys, starting at the highest village in all the Balkans, Samarina. We encountered many difficulties: we were high among the clouds and the fog, where the winds were extreme and cold. Now we are descending and descending towards the village of Kerasovo [Paraskevi].

Perhaps my sweet wife is thinking of me now, as she lies in her bed. How can she imagine where we are, how far we have wandered, and how mixed up and tangled our lives have become. I wish for her to be safe and well and for me to meet her soon.

I write all this in the moonlight.

November 15, 1940

I forgot to mention that at one point during this march my horse got stuck in the mud and fell. I dismounted quickly. Fortunately I did not get all muddy. Of course, my boots are always muddy. And when we were crossing the river my clothes got all wet. When we got to the village it was 2:00 P.M. For the first time I slept outside on woolen blankets that my assistant Pontikas laid out for me.

Crossing a river.

Thus far in my life I had thought that the creature comforts of home—like the best soft bed and exquisite food—were guaranteed, things that I had worked for and was entitled to. Little did I know that at this stage in my life I would be camped out in the cold, and not because of my own pursuit of some wild mountain adventure. There are no guarantees in life ...

Well, perhaps I write too much about food and bed; perhaps food and bed are such a part of me and this diary is beginning to sound like a lamentation for the loss of my bourgeois amenities ...

November 16, 1940

We woke up very early and marched for 11 hours; now we are getting ready to move again. My clothes are still damp ... It is an exhausting march again; we are climbing 1,000 m to the village of Fourka. Along the way, for the first time, I saw a dead Italian soldier and my hair stood on end. I thought of his parents, his brothers and sisters, his wife, who were all waiting for him while he lay flung on a mountainside in Epirus, to complete the part of the unknown soldier ... It is possible that we might meet the same fate.

Just now my colleague Sites has arrived. He is in charge of the officers' meals. He came from Fourka to our camp site, Tampouri, near the village of Zouzoulia, with pork chops, potatoes, livers, leeks and bread. I have to stop writing now so I can eat.

...

Since morning the Italians, who are close by, have been bombing us. I am diverting from the description of the march to add just these few things.

From Kerasovo we split into two units; one went ahead and we lost it. We went down to the village of Fourka and wandered around for two hours. Happily we were not discovered by enemy planes. Later we learned that we should have gone towards Tampouri. Meanwhile Sites and I ate a can of salmon and *kouramana* in secret, away from the other soldiers. I felt guilty because they had not eaten anything in 12 hours.

Finally we walked towards Tampouri, where we found the rest of our unit. We set up our tents, beds and blankets. The officers had lentil soup while the rest of the soldiers had one-fourth of a *kouramana* loaf. Tonight, my sleeping arrangements will be better than last night.

November 17, 1940

At 5:30 A.M. Officer Baltas informed me that we were going to start off very soon. By the time I divided my medical supplies (to give half to Sites), a new order came for us to stay put and wait for other orders regarding what direction to take. The Greek army has taken Koritsa [Corce] and now plans have changed. We are going to march to the front line. It is now 1:00 P.M. and we are dining on bean soup and fried livers. I am interrupting my writing to write a card to my wife.

Nov. 17
My darling,

For your birthday I wish you to be healthy and very soon to return happy to our little home so we can resume again living our old happy life.

My short note and a package will reach you hopefully in a few days, since I'm mailing them just today. I kiss you countless times ... Yours

[Later the same date]

My dearest,

It is night. There is news from London on the radio. I have your desk light covered with black paper and I write to you, my beloved.

You ask me to collect from all these people that owe you for medical services. It is very slow coming, but with the help of my father I'm getting the job done. I also ask many of our friends to help in this job. It is a lot of money that all these people owe you. How could you let them not pay you? I have become a skillful fee collector, trying to get as much as I can without hurting the feelings of any patient.

I also took care of some patients who had injuries and needed to have stitches removed. The other day some lady had just passed out and they asked me if I could administer camphor. It was very early in the morning. You see, I have become a nurse as well. I can't believe how much in demand you are and how many people miss you.

This moment Frifris[16] jumped on the desk and he is looking with his clever eyes at this letter. It is as if he wants me to send you his greetings.

How I wish I were with you to share danger and safety and to share all your worries and joys. How I wish I could cry in your arms again and fall asleep touching your hand.

Good night my boy, may God protect you.

---

16 Frifris was Dr. Electris' cat.

Your Chrysoula
Sunday night the 17th of Nov.

November 18, 1940

Yesterday I was not feeling too well—had enteritis; perhaps it was the bean soup. I fasted all day—had just a cup of milk at night. Now we are getting ready to move towards an unknown destination; the time is 8:30 P.M.

We started towards Kerasovo; I saw again the dead Italian I encountered two days ago. We descended the whole mountain all the way to the river (the one I fell in) and we were close to the entrance of the village Kerasovo when we were ordered again to turn back immediately. We started climbing up the mountain towards Tampouri, where we set our tents again. On the way back up my nurse Karamoshos and I guided a stray horse to our camp. Now I am sitting in my tent on my bed with my colleague Karasavas, my nurses and my assistant; we are waiting for food before bedtime.

"We started climbing up the mountain towards Tampouri ..." Dr. Electris is in front.

November 19, 1940

Pleasant day, sun, food and rest. The most pleasant thing, though, is that I got my salary, 3,289 dr. after taxes. I learned that I am going to get an additional salary because I am married, which will bring my total salary to 4,500–4,700 dr. I have no economic woes now, but I have to find a way to send the money to my wife and my mother.

> *Nov. 19, 1940*
>
> *No letter, not even today. Some days ago I received your letter dated Nov. 8. Since then 12 days have passed and I have not received even one card. Phaedia, I have asked you for just one little favor: please write two little words to me on a card, every day. Don't you know me? Don't you understand my agony? I know that you are busy, but writing to me two words on a card could not take more than two seconds.*
>
> *I think of you in this cold weather. The sunlit warm afternoons next to the fire don't give me pleasure any more when I think how cold you might be. These are the most worrisome and drab days of my whole life and the nights are endless. In the* Inferno *Dante says that during difficult times there is no greater sadness than feeling nostalgia for past happy moments.*
>
> *I remember the carefree days of my student life and the happiest days that I spent with you.*
>
> *My Phaedia, I long so for your love, I want to hear your voice, to see you next to me. I pray that this horrific war will soon end, that we can boot out the Italians from Albania once and for all, and you will come back to me. Then our home will be filled with joy and light and we can again resume our happy life ...*

November 20, 1940

Pleasant day, pork roast and glory to God. After lunch we were told that we were going to start off again in the morning. I learned from the accountant, Officer Gramenides, that I will get an additional 800 dr. as an officer, to improve my eating situation. It amounts up

A cartoon of the time titled "Dream" (left) and "Reality" (right).

to 5,000 dr. after taxes. So far, we are still "reservists." Now we are going to Eptahori and from there to some unknown mountain.

The Italians have been thrown out of Epirus completely, chased by our planes with assistance from British planes. When we get to Eptahori I will send 2,500 dr. to my wife and she will send 1,000 of that to my mother.

I wonder how they all are? My poor little wife, all of a sudden her life is full of worries. How I wish to see her!

November 21, 1940

We just had a reveille. We have been on this mountainside since we arrived at midnight. We got here later than we had anticipated because of the rough and irregular road. Our phalanx kept breaking up and then our group had to wait up for other groups. Our goal was to get to Eptahori, but we gave up and camped at this site. It is in an oak forest and the ground is covered with dry oak leaves. For the second time during this expedition I slept outside in the open without a tent. I stretched out on top of a woolen blanket that I took from Samarina and covered myself with my cloak. In the beginning it was very pleasant. I looked at the sky aglow with stars and it was as if I was seeing the sky for the first time. Perhaps it was a different sky than the one I used to look at when I was a child on the Black Sea, and different than the one I was used to in the city of Thessaloniki ... Perhaps I looked at the sky with a longing and a passion because, subconsciously, I was afraid that it might be my last chance to gaze at the stars ... Or perhaps it was a moment in my life when I had nothing to do but look outside of myself ...

I fell asleep as I was focusing on the most distant star that I could lay my eyes on ... but then I got very cold and desperately tried to wrap myself in my covers. Anyway, about five hours passed as I drifted in and out of sleep trying to fight the cold.

Now everyone is assembling, shifting through their things, packing, eating. I do the same. I will write to my sweet little wife. Now she will be dreaming the sweetest dream. Does she know where I am and how often I think of her? If somehow through the subconscious or telepathy we can reflect on and communicate with our loved ones, certainly she would have seen me in her dreams. My sweet wife, how much I love her!

After a few hours' walk (at about 11:00 A.M.) we finally arrived outside the village of Eptahori. I did not stay at the camp but instead took the road to the village on horseback and was there in 20 minutes. It is a fairly large village and is full of soldiers. My first job was to try to send money to my wife and my mother and send two postcards. It is very impressive how efficient the army is. It can all be accomplished through the army mail. When I finished, I was, somehow, at peace.

I went in search of food. Amazingly I found chestnuts, and I bought sheep's butter, salty cheese and village bread from a farm lady. She also gave me a cabbage and tomatoes for a gift; I gobbled up the tomatoes right on the spot! I returned to camp on my horse, eating my cabbage.

We started off again around 2:00 P.M. In the beginning the road was good, and as long as there was daylight we could see where we were going. But as night fell, hard times descended upon us: the steep roads and ravines were barely visible by the light of our torches. Many horses that were carrying supplies, and even a soldier, fell into precipitous ravines. (That wounded soldier was taken ahead to the village of Pefkophyto.) Before coming to that village, we passed a village that had my wife's name: Chrysi.

Finally, around 8:30 P.M., we arrived in the village of Pefkophyto.

What a total muddy mess! I looked around for the village priest and now I am sitting in his house near the fireplace under a pine torch light. His name is Papa Thanasis [Father Thanasis]. After I told him that I was a doctor he extended his hospitality to my colleague and myself. (Somehow, these days, being a doctor gives me great powers; I hope that will continue to hold true, especially if I have an enemy encounter.) They prepared us fried cheese and sacred bread, yogurt and mountain tea. (I forgot to write that I had an argument with Officer Christopoulos, who did not behave very well towards my colleague Sites and me; I will write later about this.)

Mail delivery center.

Soldiers attempt to rescue a pack animal that fell into a ravine.

November 22, 1940

Last night, we had not quite finished eating when an order came for all the officers to return to camp. I didn't have a chance to buy any food supplies; I wanted some walnuts, butter and honey. I'm kind of preoccupied with food, mostly because there is such a lack of it. Certainly I'm not alone in this; it is affecting everyone—big men and small, plain soldiers and officers, even the educated intellectuals and ascetic idealists who claim to be here just for Mother Greece. They all are infected by this germ called ... well, called "hunger." Those who claim that they are not, they are just plain lying.

Anyway, my job at hand was to load my colleagues' and my gear on a donkey already loaded with other camp supplies. We then camped two miles from the village. We covered ourselves well and went to sleep.

This morning we woke up before the crack of dawn and got our things together. There was spaghetti and bread to eat and I had a whole "mess pot."

At 11:00 A.M. we were on our way again. We arrived in the village of Myrovlitis. The river Sarandaporos runs parallel to it. The village is deserted; rumor has it that the villagers were traitors.

Just now the wireless field phone announced that the GREEK ARMY GOT INTO KORITSA!

As far as Captain Christopoulos is concerned, I should note here that he is a man of not-too-good family upbringing; this, perhaps, can explain his behavior. From the first day I met him, he has wanted to prove his superiority and his intelligence. I think he derives pleasure and sadistic enjoyment from seeing a doctor or other educated person struggling with hardships. My colleague Sites and I got an extra horse from some friends in the 4th Artillery to carry our supplies. Officer Christopoulos threw all our supplies off the horse and started hollering at us. When I stood up to him, he threatened me directly with his gun. In the morning I had to let my colonel know that if something was to happen to me, Christopoulos would be to blame.

Today I will send a letter to my wife and a request to headquarters to have my salary transferred directly to her.

Nov. 22, 1940
My beloved Phaedia,
At this moment as I write to you I can hear the church bells.
People are celebrating, crazy with joy, because we captured
Koritsa. The houses and stores are all decorated with flags.
I can only imagine the great joy of all the soldiers at the front.
My Phaedia, every victory and every piece of good news fills me
with happiness and hope that our parting will be short. My love,
I long for you so much.
The doorbell and the phone have been ringing constantly from
a stream of people announcing this happy event. They all send
their love to you.

November 24, 1940

On Saturday morning at around 7:00 A.M. we started for the village of Paliohori. A light rain was falling, and I made a makeshift raincoat out of my tent as I walked with the commanding unit. Sites had gone ahead with the colonel.

The rain was getting heavier and more annoying, and in a moment of long-forgotten boyish passion for incautious pioneering, I decided to ride ahead of the artillery and arrive at our destination at the same time as the colonel.

After I passed the 4th Artillery, I did not run into the colonel and his group; so, foolishly, I tried to head to-

Alexandros D. Alexandrakis: "This way we fought—1941."

ward our destination by orienting myself using different landmarks, riding ahead of everyone else. I was detached from our unit and I should have waited there for them, but my big ego, my attitude that I could do anything, and my terrible impatience gave me the illusion that I was invincible and that I would arrive at our destination sooner than anyone else.

I paid dearly for my reckless adventurism.

Before I realized it, I found myself at a great altitude. Meanwhile the rain had stopped, but the trail was becoming more and more difficult; I had to dismount and drag my poor horse by the reins. We must have been at about 1,800 m judging from the amount of snow on the surrounding mountains.

We finally came to a cross trail, but I did not know which road to take ...

My boyish gutsy attitude deserted me. I felt my age, far removed from the wild soul of youth, I felt that I was a civilian again, who long ago had abandoned outdoor adventures for storm-tight roofs and creature comforts. Besides, I was in a war and at any time I could have an enemy encounter.

I could not get my courage up to walk ahead, so, I hung around the trail crossing and waited, hoping that my unit would show up, but to no avail. They must have been a long ways away ...

At about 4:00 P.M. it was getting dark, and I had to think hard and fast about what I had to do. The solution was to camp at that spot. Fortunately, I had my horse, Lemargos, loaded with some hay for him and a blanket and some food for me.

My first thought was to take off all my clothes, because I was soaked from top to bottom. I was so nervous that I used up 15 matches before I could start a fire. Then, I walked to the edge of the mountain and called out for our unit, hoping that someone would hear me. Alas, I was deserted; or, more accurately, I had detached myself from the unit and was responsible for being lost. Thoughts of my house, my wife, everyone flashed through my mind.

With some branches and my raincoat I made myself a spot to lie down. I put half the blanket on the bottom and started drying my socks by the fire. After I finished, I started slowly nibbling on bread and cheese, trying not to fall asleep, because I was worried about wolves. In my pockets I found some chestnuts from Eptahori and started roasting them one by one.

I will never forget that night and all that went through my mind. There was a time in the heart of my youth when I longed to be alone, and sought solitude with all my might; there was a time when rising in the wilderness looking for adventure meant the ultimate freedom, the consummate path to manhood. Now, however, I'm tied to home and wife, a human bond so sweet and strong that it kills a man's wild soul. This aloneness I once sought seems unbearable now. How terrible it is to be alone in a forest!

After my chestnuts were gone, exhaustion overcame me and I started dozing off. Occasionally I would overcome my sleepiness, open up my eyes and stare at the sky, clear now and full of shining bright stars. Looking at the stars would invigorate me for a moment, as though their light energy would transport me back to a time not too long ago when my world seemed so safe and predictable. But soon I would again feel enervated and scared; at least I was fortunate that the rain had stopped.

My horse, Lemargos, who was tied to a tree and eating his hay, was my only companion for the night.

I have never felt closer to an animal. He was closer to me than my cat Frifris. I think he sensed that, too, because he came nearer to me and I could feel his breath on my face. I took a few sips from a

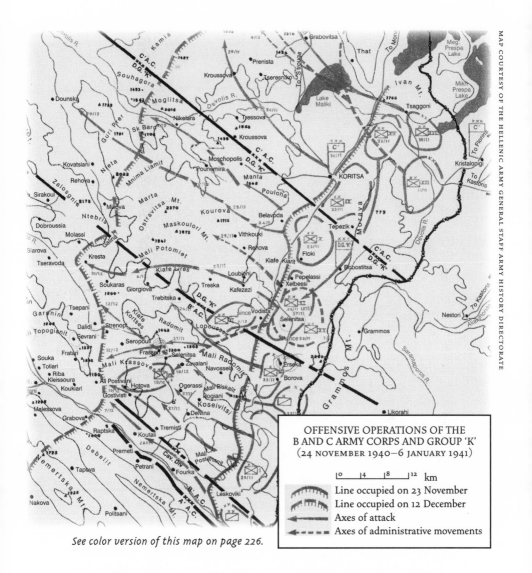

MAP COURTESY OF THE HELLENIC ARMY GENERAL STAFF ARMY HISTORY DIRECTORATE

OFFENSIVE OPERATIONS OF THE
B AND C ARMY CORPS AND GROUP 'K'
(24 NOVEMBER 1940–6 JANUARY 1941)

0   4   8   12 km

Line occupied on 23 November
Line occupied on 12 December
Axes of attack
Axes of administrative movements

See color version of this map on page 226.

drink that I had made from the brandy I had in my canteen and the
honey I had bought in Pefkophyto. Having Lemargos there made
me feel more secure; I had the sure feeling that he would protect me
from wolves and enemies alike, and so we fell asleep, he standing up
and I curled up near a tree and covered with my cloak.

Winter 1940: Dr. Electris is seated on a stretcher underneath his tent. Behind him is his horse, Lemargos.

November 25, 1940

The morning found us and cloaked us with fog. It was 7:00 A.M. Sunday (a fact that I had almost forgotten), and there were no signs of any of our troops anywhere. I started a fire and let Lemargos loose to graze on whatever he could find. I toasted some bread, ate it with butter and sipped some of my special drink. Periodically I would walk to the edge of the mountain and call for my unit. Every so often I could hear very remote voices, way too remote. Thick fog would cover the mountain off and on.

Just now the sun is shining and I am finishing my notes. I'll wait a little longer (about an hour) and if my unit does not show up, I will go in search of them.

...

When I could no longer hear anyone, I decided to load Lemargos and start walking downhill. We walked in sort of a trance for a very long time. To get out of that state I started talking to Lemargos.

The majesty of Gramos Mountain.

PHOTO: GEO MAGAZINE, SEPTEMBER 13, 2004

I explained to him about the rekindling of my pioneering spirit that got us into the predicament that we were in. He shook his head with understanding, explaining to me that my actions were not so reckless but only brave and noble, like those of his other horsemen masters before me. I don't recall how many hours passed thus talking and walking, but at some point I realized that I was at the same path where I had started a day earlier. I was in the middle of a huge pine forest. There were signs of abandoned camps, makeshift seats and tables built from logs and branches, indispensable items for an army camp. In and around that camp I got mixed up again and felt desperately lost and alone. By chance I took a path that was running parallel to the river. I think I was very lucky; suddenly I saw a little old man with his horse crossing the river. How encouraged one gets encountering another human soul after 30 hours of isolation at high altitude. When I am at camp I always think of home and wife and family. But when I found myself alone on the mountain, with what longing did I think of the camp, my assistant Pontikas, my nurses and my colleagues!

Finally old Mr. Vasilios Athanasiou from Kolokythou guided Lemargos and me to the road that all the transfer supply trucks were traveling on. After thanking him and giving him my card and one of my jackets, I followed the trucks. I walked for another 20 km and arrived in Gramos, the last village on Greek soil. There I met with Officer Tosonides of the Transfer Division. He gave Lemargos grain and me bread to eat! What treats!

After an hour's rest, we started climbing—again—a three-hour ascent to 2,500 m. Then we started going downward into Albanian lands: a three-hour descent. Fortunately, there were not many rocks in the road, and at around 9:00 P.M. we arrived in the village of Skorovod [Skorovat].

The colonel reprimanded me for my disappearance and detachment from our unit. I tried to apologize as much as I could. Tosonides (a lawyer from Thessaloniki) and I spent the night in a house, so we did not get too cold. The rest of our soldiers stayed in tents. I forgot to mention earlier that before we left Gramos I had my horse outfitted with special mountain-climbing horseshoes that had fallen off a mule.

I organized all my supplies in a house set aside for the officers. I then went to another house, where I had some milk and settled down. I had my picture taken with a beard and then I shaved. I did

PHOTO COURTESY OF THE HELLENIC WAR DIRECTORATE

Barbering at the front.

not shave my mustache however. In this house I bathed for the first time with warm water, because in my underwear (which I am having washed) I discovered a few lice.

It is now 7:30 P.M. We will have something to eat and then sleep. Tomorrow we will have some milk. I wrote to my wife and my mother.

November 27, 1940

Yesterday we started off very early in the morning. The wilderness of the mountain passages had given way to a sun-filled, gentle landscape where the earth was soft and the paths easy to walk on. The cold mountain winds, though, kept blowing angrily upon us.

We passed many villages with mixed populations: Moslem and Orthodox. As the Greek army was advancing, many of the villagers and their animals were returning to their homes.

The truth is that the Moslems oppress the Christians, so perhaps many of the Moslems had decided to leave when the Greek forces were passing through.

As we were passing from the village of Selenitsa [Selenice], there was an air raid involving about 25 Italian airplanes. Some of the bombs fell on the village and four people were injured. One hit our unit and killed three mules and wounded one soldier on the head. At that moment we were in the forest and we could hear the explosions.

We arrived in the village of Seliberda around 5:00 P.M. I spent the night in a regular tent with Officers Eliades and Tosonides and my nurses. My colleague Sites stayed in another tent, on a faraway hill. I did not like his behavior towards me today. He attended the soldier who was wounded during the bombing and, not having his medical supplies close at hand, he sent his nurse to find supplies and the nurse asked me for my supplies. I told his nurse that I would have preferred for him to run a little further and get Sites' supplies, since they were not that much further off and I am very particular about my equipment. I don't know how the nurse related all of that to Sites, but he complained openly to the colonel, saying that I refused to give him medical supplies! He was out of line complaining. He is a strange fellow, always sucking up to the colonel; he reminds me of a court jester! I will express to him my dismay later on. From now on I have to watch out for him, and maintain a more "reserved" posture. Now that I think about it, it seems to me that he caused the whole incident with Lieutenant Christopoulos two days ago. All these dealings with people are quite annoying. I thought that I had passed the stage in my life that I had to focus on tiresome and sophomoric behaviors. But perhaps I was to blame as well. I'm always picky about my supplies ... and war does not allow for idiosyncratic and neurotic attitudes.

Within the next couple of days we will assume fighting positions.

November 28, 1940

Yesterday was extremely cold and [I] could not find a way to stay warm. I woke up in the middle of the night freezing and covered up with my cloak, but even that did not help. This morning was sunny but penetratingly cold. I had milk and toast, butter and biscuits and marmalade from my sweet little wife. I hope that in Thessaloniki they have plenty of everything now that the British are there.[17]

At around 8:00 P.M. last night, in the presence of an army priest, many officers from infantry and the commanding division of our unit, Colonel Drungas, Officers Loukakis and Anagnostou, my colleagues Sites, Samaras and I took the oath of the "reservist" officer. After that, about 8:05, we listened to the news from London. At that moment my thoughts flew to my home and my sweet wife, who most certainly was sitting in the small chair next to the radio, having me as her only thought. This gives me courage for the bad times and deprivation that we have to go through.

Eating is again very irregular and, as always, something to complain about. Yesterday we were given just a fifth of *kouramana* for the whole day; we eat food with no salt and we do really miss salt. Sometimes we eat meat without *kouramana*. Miraculously, the other day I had some milk!

---

17 The British were in Thessaloniki as undercover forces in civilian clothes.

In the morning my hostler and I went to the village and tried to find someone to wash my clothes; that was an unsuccessful waste of time. The only thing I accomplished was to buy half a loaf of corn bread for ten drachmas.

Now I'm sitting in my tent waiting for lunch. I am not speaking to Sites because he did not behave like a good colleague; he is worse than Lieutenant Christopoulos, who does not have even half his education. He is an egoist and an opportunist.

Today I have completed a whole month in the army, a whole month of walking and marching and more marching. It seems to me that we will be marching until all the Italians are gone from Albanian soil. Perhaps today or tomorrow we will occupy our positions. The 4th Artillery has taken its position at the front. But it is entirely possible that we will start marching again, because the Italians are deserting their positions everywhere.

At the village I sent letters via Koritsa to my wife.

November 30, 1940

Yesterday we started walking towards the first line village of Panarita [Panarit]. We passed through a Greek village and finally camped. The command unit is about 1 km behind the 3rd Artillery, which has occupied a fighting position. When we awoke—at the usual time—everything was covered with snow. We are getting ready to move again. We are marching back, toward a village (as a reserve unit). We are supposed to be attached to the 50th Unit. If we can finally find the 50th Unit, perhaps I will meet some people I know—like Demetrios Layias. When we camp I will write a letter and send it home to my wife, my sweet little wife.

December 2, 1940

After receiving an order two days ago we started, as I wrote, to walk in a rearward direction until it got dark. We camped near the river of the village Lisabonia. Christopoulos went to the command (division) to report on the situation. Unhappily, when he returned he disappointed us all because he brought new orders for us to start marching again, immediately and in a different direction. We were supposed to start marching on again at 10:00 P.M.

I, however, was unscathed by this unpleasant situation and was the happiest man in the world, because Lieutenant Christopoulos (whose bad manners I have forgotten) brought me letters from my wife and my sister-in-law Nitsa, two from my father and one from my mother-in-law. I cannot describe the excitement and joy I felt for my wife's letters, my sweet little girl who has been left alone without my hugs and kisses. She sends me money and packages, which I haven't received. I will search for all of that, but I will send the money back, as I don't need it.

After reading the letters and without a pause I wrote a bunch of postcards. Unfortunately, I had no idea when, where, or how I could mail them.

Around 10:00 P.M. we started getting ready to move. It was half raining and half snowing when we finally started off. We walked in some new direction until 10:00 A.M. on Dec. 1st. We passed the river Osoum [Apsos] and a bridge and arrived at the village Orgotsika—with Greek inhabitants—in all seven houses. Fortunately, I

A machine-gun crew in snow-covered terrain.

had saved in my mess pot some boiled pork that was given to us at the camp near the village of Katsiny. It tasted so good eating it as I walked in the snows of the forest of the mountain Kiafentini at an altitude of 1,305 m.

A Greek artillery piece.

The Italians are well reinforced and wedged in the opposite mountain. Our battery will start firing at them around 2:00 P.M. For us, though, there is an order to move again in a new direction as a reserve attachment.

I got birthday wishes from my wife, Aunt Mahi and Nitsa for November. My birthday, though, is on the 17th of December, not November. I have only told it to her once and most probably she has forgotten it. I'm not going to mention it to her and upset her.

In Orgotsika many of the officers were guests of the villagers, so we slept in houses instead of at the camp. I slept like a corpse after being up for 28 hours straight. In the morning I finally succeeded in having my clothes washed. Now I am sitting in front of a fireplace and am writing these lines. It is 11:30 and I am going to go check on the colonel. My host's name is Petros M. Vasiliades. His address is Erseke, Kolonis, village of Orgotsika. When, fate willing, I get back to Thessaloniki, I will send his wife, Eleni, a dress. (c/o Simeonides Bros. merchants, Erseke Kolonis, for Petros Vasiliades, Orgotsika village)

December 5, 1940

The past two nights I spent in the village taking care of the colonel, who was sick. It was not a bad time. Now I am back at camp, having slept fairly well, sharing my tent with my hostler. Last night I again experienced great joy as I received the first package from my wife. She sent me that long-sleeve sweater that I watched her knitting while I was still at home. I know with how much love she tried to make me something with her own two hands and when I got it last night I couldn't wait to put it on. I think it transmitted to me the warmth of her body, and her candy gave me the taste of the sweetness of her kisses. I also got some handkerchiefs and some special sutures I had requested. Today I answered my father-in-law and sent a card to my sister Popi. Presently I am in my tent. I don't know when we are going to move again. I hope I get some more letters. Adjutant Iasonides is supplying me with sugar. For lunch we had lentil soup.

December 8, 1940

On the morning of the 6th, in a cataclysmic rain, we left our camp outside the village of Orgotsika. We walked all day, through mostly passable places, and crossed the river at least 25 times. At night we arrived outside the village of Fraseri [Frasher] and tried to camp in the hard rain. Pontikas and I set up our tent, placed branches in the bottom and blankets on top. I cannot complain because I had a very warm and sweet sleep. It rained all night but we did not get wet. On the morning of the 7th we started off on a climb towards the village of Kensibasi [Qeshibesh], where we gathered again in order to continue to our final destination. We walked for two and a half hours and arrived opposite the Italian lines. It was the first time I saw our guns firing. Tomorrow we will participate as well.

Now in my tent, I have lit a candle atop my mess pot; I am reclining and write to my wife, my mother and Nitsa—postcards for everyone, to be sent every day by Sergeant Kontos who will go to headquarters. I'm going to have some tea and go to bed.

December 9, 1940

It is a very rainy day. The water has penetrated us from top to bottom and from bottom to top. If the war with guns is horrible, the war against nature is equally bad. Besides, deprivation is becoming definitely noticeable. We have no *kouramana* and have not eaten anything cooked in three days. We cannot light any fires because we are worried that we will be a target for the enemy.

It is a matter of great endurance and suffering for the officers and much more for our poor soldiers. About an hour ago some *kouramanes* arrived from far away—a distance of two days' climb.

From our position, near Kakosi, we are starting to fire at the enemy in their fortified stronghold below the opposite village. From the observatory I can watch both our batteries firing continuously. Our command headquarters is at a distance of one hour from the observatory. We can just see it across from us, but it would take one hour to reach it on foot. The *Stathmos*[18] medical headquarters is in

18 *Stathmos* means "station" in Greek.

the command unit as well. I am in a small tent; however, all my supplies and equipment are outside and getting wet. I have no idea how our unit is going to attack if it becomes necessary ...

Today with the *kouramanes*, Tosonides brought me four letters from my wife, a letter from my sister Evridiki and one from my friend Antonis. They were such a relief and tonic in the loneliness and deprivation of these days. We have to wait and see how long this tormented adventure is going to last.

I heard that we are going to stay here for at least 2–3 days. We all have to endure. If Klissoura does not fall we are all going to suffer, most of all, though, our soldiers who are fighting near the Klissoura area.

Today I saw a soldier picking up the crumbs and peel of the piece of cheese I had just eaten. Yesterday, as I was standing by the observatory, an officer passing with his unit came close to me and looked at the piece of *kouramana* and cheese I was about to eat. I gave him half of what I was eating and wished I had more to give to his soldiers. Alas, this deprivation and the horrible winter will break us all down.

It is now 7:30 P.M. How delicious this warm mushy rice and spaghetti are after so many days of only *kouramana* and a cheese crumb. We are eating and hoping that the food will not disappear. It has rejuvenated us and warmed up our bodies. How many times I did not appreciate the food at home and complained about Aunt Mahi's spaghetti. From these deprivations in the army how many lessons we are learning! I wish to get home soon and hug and kiss everyone, even my house if that is possible.

December 11, 1940

Yesterday the weather improved to the point that we almost dried out. I had Pontikas make my tent again with hay for a pillow. We spread the blankets accordingly. Tosonides brought us two butchered oxen that we split up among the battery. My colleague Sites was responsible for cooking the oxen for the 3rd and 4th units. I do not speak to Sites anymore; on the other hand, Officer Christopoulos has changed his behavior towards me and treats me with respect. (This army is making me behave like a schoolboy, choosing groups of friends I like and not speaking to others; it is all so petty, but that's the social life of the army ...)

I was responsible for cooking the oxen for the officers. I added to my assistants a cook by the name of George Ziogas who had just come back from the hospital, where I had sent him earlier for treatment of burns on his leg. He made the most delicious soup from the oxen head and cooked spaghetti in the broth. I was totally stuffed after just sampling the livers, the broth and the meat, so I saved my spaghetti for breakfast. We made *patsa*[19] soup with the hooves.

In the morning we had tea, so I filled my canteen with broth for later. For lunch we will have bean soup. It is beginning to sound again like a gastronomic diary, but food is important, especially when it comes down to survival ...

Meanwhile, yesterday, the battle was raging on the height opposite us. Our 50th regiment with great difficulty crossed the river and occupied certain positions. We had tremendous losses. One of the units (a battalion) was decimated. There were many dead and wounded. The points that were captured were taken with fixed bayonets.

Today a brigade will arrive for reinforcement. Yesterday our artillery was firing till nightfall. All day long the enemy, who are very well covered with many nests of artillery and four 75s, were firing at us. The shells would whistle by and explode all around and up to 500 m behind our unit. Many of them fell on our artillery. At night all was quiet, but once in a while an exploding gun would bring us back to our senses assuring us that the danger was near.

After dinner I sat around with the officers for about an hour, then I went to bed and slept, all warm and dry.

---

19 Typical Greek soup, usually made from pig hooves.

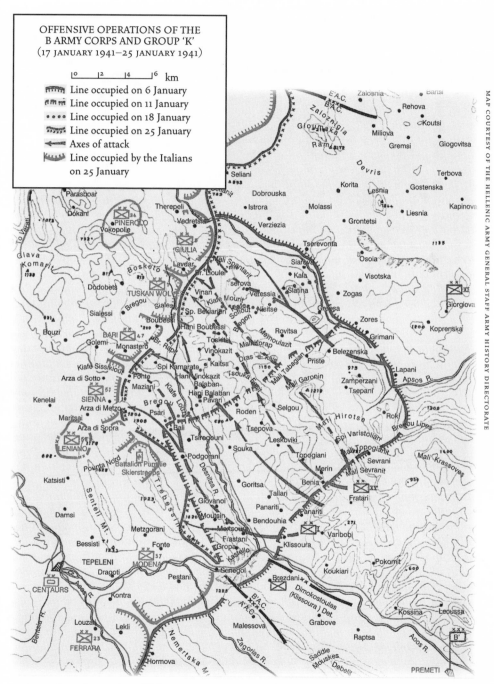

OFFENSIVE OPERATIONS OF THE
B ARMY CORPS AND GROUP 'K'
(17 JANUARY 1941–25 JANUARY 1941)

0   2   4   6 km

~~~~~ Line occupied on 6 January
~~~~~ Line occupied on 11 January
••••• Line occupied on 18 January
~~~~~ Line occupied on 25 January
←─── Axes of attack
~~~~~ Line occupied by the Italians
      on 25 January

See color version of this map on page 227.

"My colleague Sites was responsible for cooking the oxen ..."

December 12, 1940

When we awoke everything was covered with snow, but the sun was up. By 10:00 A.M. it was cloudy again. I readied some checks, so I could send some money home.

> *Dec. 12*
>
> *My Phaedia,*
>
> *Don't worry about my safety during the air raids. I am very brave and can take care of myself. You should take care to be safe and to write me every day. I can die from agony waiting for your news; though I have not received your letters, I'm sure you are writing them. Let me know if I can come and meet you somewhere. I kiss you.*

December 14, 1940

Two days ago the sun shining on the freshly fallen snow was so splendid that we forgot the perils of war. We even took pictures.

The beauty of nature has such an empowering effect on me; I could be in the midst of the worst life experience, but just a glistening raindrop or the petal of an almond blossom will lift my spirit. Perhaps I have trained myself to look for these instant joys when I'm down, it is so much a part of my person, my being, just like breathing ...

Like all pleasures, the beautiful morning was too short, and in the afternoon the weather turned nasty with an ice storm; we also started to feel the lack of supplies again.

Last night I had a nightmare; I dreamt that my wife had some sort of an eye disease and I had a 24-hour leave and went to find her. I could not find her, as hard as I tried. I was so worried that I was crying in my sleep, and I could sense it. I was under the influence of that bad dream the whole day.

Dreams are powerful experiences. Perhaps they are flawed thoughts or memories of thoughts or experiences that randomly assemble themselves haphazardly and take over your being and control it when it is in a weakened state, emotionally down or sleeping. When I'm awake my will can cause and empower the positive. Perhaps dreams are flawed telepathic receptions of mangled thoughts, interrupted by static (like the wireless) from people who are thinking of you. When you are in a weakened state, as I've been, they overtake you.

Anyway, that bad dream haunted me the whole day. How is my sweet wife? Am I going to get a letter from her today when Tosonides comes? How much I miss her, how much I wish to see my parents, my neighbors, my *parea*, my patients, my cat Frifris—all that I call home, my heart and soul and essence of being.

...

Today we have had many undesirable visits from enemy planes. We are expecting *kouramana* but don't know whether we will get any. We are going to have boiled meat with broth; but how can one eat without bread?[20]

---

20 Bread is the most important part of a Greek meal.

Just now my nurses have brought me a huge squash from the nearby village. They are going to bake it in the fire. It is going to be terrific!

We have another big problem: half of our animals have died, and if we capture the village across from us, it will be very hard to move. We hope that some other units will help us take over the positions across the way and chase the Italians away. As for me, I hope that my love will give me courage to endure all these deprivations and adversities.

December 17, 1940

Today is my birthday, a pleasant day, despite the subzero temperatures.

Perhaps this day reflects the point I'm at in life. The present situation, this war, like the severe cold weather, is a very unpleasant reality; however, looking at the overall picture of my life, the sun is shining high and in my thirty-two years I have many achievements that I have to celebrate: I survived being a refugee, survived the hard work of school, and I have found my calling, healing the ill, taking care of the needy—medicine. I am blessed to have been given the opportunity to combine my passions with all the scientific disciplines I'm interested in as a single profession, or perhaps an art. In medicine I can utilize pure science and intuition and, possibly philosophical thinking, mixed with some folk wisdom.

I can thus satisfy my moral and ethical needs for human compassion and also stimulate my intellectual and spiritual life through my profession.

Also, I'm twice blessed, because I met my golden angel, my Chrysoula. Perhaps I'm an optimist; I see the bright side of things, and if I'm lucky and can hold my dream tight to my heart and soul—always being connected to it, always finding solace in it—perhaps it will come true, and this war will end, like the freezing weather.

Now to some more mundane things:

I got my December salary: 4,923 dr. and the remnant of November's. I received two cards from Chrysoula and one from my sister

Evridiki and a letter from my father. Today I ordered my officer's cap and greatcoat. Last night I went to the village of Kakos to see some patients from the artillery. We have stayed in this camp too long—almost ten days—and we are totally frozen. (Today's food: omelets, soup, rice, boiled head of oxen.)

December 19, 1940

The days pass; events are almost indistinguishable from day to day. The only difference is the cold, which is getting worse and worse, almost unbearable. These days all the officers from the command unit get together to talk about our lives (Colonel Drungas, Officers Baltas, Christopoulos, Anagnostou, Iliades and I). I am very impressed with the discussions I have with the colonel. On just about every subject he is very well read and educated. I admire and respect him immensely. I consider him as close as a brother.

In these discussions I satisfy my intellectual needs, but nothing can push away from my mind my sweet little wife, my happiness that I have finally found after so many years of searching.

Meeting her somehow changed my life's focus. I—who selflessly did things for others, many times not thinking of myself, giving, healing bodies and souls—suddenly experienced the feeling of the ultimate pleasure of being with another person, body and soul. It is almost like some kind of an addiction to the eternal joy of being with this other person that makes me want to experience it over and over again. It is a primitive, a primeval, need to keep experiencing this happiness, a happiness as great as that of Adam's when he encountered Eve!

We barely had a chance to even take a breath of this happiness before I was obliged to go and live away from her, with just the solace of her memory. My golden Chrysoula, she did not even have a chance to learn how to love me and I have gone away from her. For me at least her love is my hope in this expedition, it gives me strength to withstand our parting and all the difficulties. I am serene because I know without any doubt that I belong to her; I can say that I am the one with the greatest benefit from her love, and

THE EPIC OF 1940: HISTORICAL & ETHNOLOGICAL SOCIETY OF GREECE NATIONAL HISTORICAL MUSEUM

The battle of the giants in the narrows of Klissoura.

my poor darling is at a loss without me. I am indebted to her forever. I will try—if I survive—to be faithful to her (as I have been up to now) and will create for her a life the way she dreamt of it.

Today I stayed in my tent longer than usual (though the weather is great). This way my feet are not freezing and I have a chance to write while my spirit is calm. Up to now they have not succeeded in getting us the regulation tents, and I think that I will never sleep on a bed ever. Happily, my endurance is still good.

Our hopes are that, perhaps soon, we will defeat the enemy, whose troops have been barricaded on the mountain across from us and who, a week ago, caused many dead and wounded in our 50th Unit (perhaps due to a mistake of our commanders). Our forces are also closing in around Klissoura, which has a direct impact on our front. Let's hope that the holidays will come under better conditions.

It is about 11:00 and it is time I get out of my "hole" to do my patient rounds.

December 22, 1940

I sent 500 dr. to my mother with Nikolaides. This way she will afford the ingredients for *vasilopites*.[21] I also sent cards with wishes to my sweet wife. I hope that they'll get everything in time for New Year's Eve. The last three days passed without snow and with sunshine and listlessness.

December 23, 1940

At this moment—9:30 A.M.—the general attack against the enemy position across from us is commencing from all directions. We hope that it will fall and we will have a Merry Christmas. Mr. Tosonides and I are in the colonel's tent and we are waiting ... I am not well, I have enteritis. (To get well I will go on strict diet for two days.) Being sick is nothing in comparison to the raging battle. We are all keeping our hopes up.

Last night it stormed and all was white, covered with snow. Now the sky couldn't be any clearer; it is a godly, joyous day—but an ungodly bloody battle is raging. Overwhelming sounds of guns and explosions surround us.

December 24, 1940

Last night I had one of the greatest surprises. I received three packages all at the same time: flannel underwear, hand-knit socks, a cap, gloves and two huge boxes of sweets. I learned that, unfortunately, what I sent home had gone to the wrong address. Today I will write letters to all. Christmas is tomorrow and our predicament has not changed. The enemy height has not fallen, and I still cannot eat a thing.

---

21 Traditional New Year's sweet bread, with a coin hidden inside for good luck.

Mail delivery.

Dec. 24

My adored Phaedia,

Christmas Eve ... At this moment children have come to sing carols for the first time at our house. What joy I would have experienced if things were different. I want to send you this long letter I've written, but I'm afraid you won't get it, like all the other letters. I write to you only that I miss you very much and I pray that you return healthy so we can celebrate together next year. I kiss you countless times.

PHOTO BY ALEXANDER LINDSAY

A hand-drawn Christmas card from Chrysoula. See color version on page 224.

December 26, 1940

Christmas came and went with snow and lots of mud. My only
pleasure was that I luckily found a spare moment to write to my
sweet wife and to my mother and brother and my friend Antonis.
The letters were sent with Mr. Tosonides. I also gave him 1,000 dr.
to send to my wife. Today we set up a regular tent, which I share
with Nikolaides and the communications officer. I am in there with
my bed and all of my medical supplies and equipment; I don't know
how long we are going to be here, but tonight I am going to sleep in
a bed! This moment, as I write sitting on my BED, is 10:00 P.M.

Dec. 26
My Phaedia,
    May 1941 bring you soon to our little nest, near your love who
is passionately waiting for you.
Countless kisses.

PHOTO BY DR. THEODORE ELECTRIS

December 26, 1940: "Christmas came and went with snow and lots of mud."

December 27, 1940

I got rid of Pontikas, my groom, because he would not do the work the way I wanted him to. Many times he pretended that he did not understand what I was telling him. I hired someone from Halkidiki temporarily to try him out. I had him shave, wash and boil his clothes.

These days I am also very sad because my horse Lemargos has died. I was so used to him and I will forever feel guilty for abusing him by overloading him and dragging him up and down impassable ravines and rivers of mud and frozen mountainsides. He was made for nobler things, he could not withstand all the difficulties of this torturous expedition. I will certainly miss him and as long as I live he will live with me forever, because I will carry him in my heart ...

This evening we have a guest officer in our tent. Because we have no room, he will necessarily sleep on the stretcher, which will be set in the middle of the tent over the brazier, so he will keep warm at the same time.

Tonight, listening to the radio again, the thoughts of my sweet wife, my home and all overtook me.

December 28, 1940

It is 7:30 P.M. and I am not feeling well. I will fold my washed clothes, have some tea and quinine and go to bed. This morning I went to Kakos for patient rounds. I was not feeling well, even when I was trying to buy vinegar and onions to bring back to the cook at camp. He needed these special things in order to cook a hare that two soldiers killed for the officers. I'm glad that I already had sent the letters home.

December 29, 1940

I am definitely feeling better. I ate with such an appetite! The cook and I prepared the hare and everyone raved about it. I also ate some halvah that Mr. Tosonides brought back from the supply headquarters. Mr. Tosonides is going to be our guest in our tent tonight; he'll use our very special heated-stretcher guest bed.

He was not able to send my money to my wife because our divisional commander had already left for Trebiska [Trebicke]. So, unfortunately, my mother and wife will be without money for two months.

I forgot to write that two days ago I had the unfortunate job of beating one of the soldiers ... He had been sent to the gun supply headquarters to bring ammunition. He returned two days later than the other soldiers and without ammunition. His story was that as he was returning he fell, dropped the ammunition down a ravine and broke his arm. He had his shirtsleeves off, hanging loose and his arm tied against his body and he was whimpering about his pain. Somehow, my medical practice has taught me how to read people's faces. It is my first step, in any examination, so ingrained in my practice it is almost a reflex: the patient's face, his or her eyes, lead me to my first hypothesis; second step, the stethoscope ... Well, at first glance, it appeared that something was not right, and that "something" turned out to be the soldier's story; on closer examination it all proved to be a big lie, so he got a few slaps in the face for a gift ... for trying to fool us.

The most important happening today was the final fall of the mountain across from us: Mali Sevranit,[22] that tragic mountain that our 50th Unit tried to climb after crossing the river Apsos. This time, however it was surrounded from behind, as well, by the infantry battalion of another unit, so the Italians retreated from 1220[23] and beyond. At this moment, about 5:00 P.M., over and beyond our unit a huge air battle is taking place.

December 31, 1940

The last day of the year! I straightened out the tent, changed, shaved and cut my hair. I put on the heavy woolen socks that my wife made. I've never been with my wife on a New Year's Eve and I'm sorry for that, and I know that she is sorry that I am so far away—if only she knew how really far away ... The last evening of the bad year will be celebrated by all the officers tonight. I hope that the New Year will be auspicious for all.

Today I schemed a way of sending some money home even if it's only a little. I gave somebody named Yiannis Theodoridhis 200 dr.; his parents in turn will pay the money back to my wife in Thessaloniki. So with the 500 dr. that I sent with Karamoshos I will have sent them at least 700 dr., better than nothing ...

Now I am smoking my 6th cigarette since I left for the front.

Time: 10:20 P.M.

I listen to the news using headphones. My thoughts, though, are of my sweet wife and of home, if only I could fly there like radio waves ...

Later I receive a card from my wife and my mother-in-law Thelxiopi. I learn that they have received my money orders of Nov. 15 and 17.

A very funny thing happened earlier tonight. Just before the news, I had gone out into the woods for that special business ... When I got back to my tent I tried to take care of some paperwork.

---

22 Mountain by the town of Sevran.
23 A military designation for a certain position.

PHOTO FROM DIARY DOCUMENTS

Smoking was a rare indulgence for Dr. Electris (center).

I had some unsigned checks and other papers that needed some attention. As I looked in my pockets for the two checks, I could only find one. Then I remembered that when I was out in the woods doing my business I had searched my pockets for some soft paper. Immediately I returned to the woods with a flashlight and happily found my check, ah, a touch wrinkled ... I took care of it, appropriately disinfected it and signed it.

It is 11:00 P.M. it is time I join the rest of the officers for discussion, then when I return I will write to my sweet wife.

January 1, 1941

I do not know why, but the day passed somewhat unpleasantly. First I had an argument with Sublieutenant Veziroglou because he sent us very poor quality meat. Then I was annoyed with Sergeant Ioannides, the wireless operator. It's not enough that he is permitted to share our tent since we're short of space, but he wants my four nurses and my hostler to cater to him and his assistant. I had to straighten him out about all that, and when he talked back to me I had to remind him that he was talking to an officer. Despite all these disturbances, I could go to sleep and rest O.K. at night.

Included in a package was this card from Chrysoula to Dr. Electris. It reads:

My dearest Phaedia,

    Our little house I have decorated with chrysanthemums. On your desk your papers are they way you left them.

    My Phaedia, my thoughts are always with you. I think continuously that I'll see you and I'll hear your voice. The days are endless and the nights even longer—the hours do not pass, indeed, even if one counts them. How I long for you. I did not know that I loved you so much!

Thousands of kisses,

your Chrysoula

January 2, 1941

In the morning I finished an extensive letter to my wife and wrote to my uncle Theodore in Katahas and to my wife's uncle Xenophon. Then I went to headquarters to take care of some professional business. There I received an order to get down to the XI B chamber of the 65th Artillery Unit where some serious accident had occurred with a gun and there were some critical injuries. Indeed we had three soldiers injured from fragments of shells. One died from a fractured skull and two others received serious injuries in the head, chest and arms. It is terrible to have people die from such an accident, as if dying in battle is not enough.

Death is never a pretty sight. As a doctor I've lived with it, fought it, wished it at times for some, but never, never got used to it … perhaps I never will, it is so antithetical to my nature, especially when, like today, young people are involved. It's such a waste.

The mailman has not come yet, but I found a way to send my mail with a soldier who was going to the division command headquarters. I'm looking forward to the mailman coming—I need a pleasant surprise on this sad day.

I forgot to mention that I kept a fragment of the shell from one of the injured. I worked so intensely on him and was relieved to leave with at least the hope that somehow he was going to make it.

January 3, 1941

Indeed as I predicted and anticipated, I was rained upon with mail, letters, cards and gifts from my wife, my aunt-in-law Andromahi, my sisters-in-law Elli and Nitsa, my sister Evridiki and my mother. I got socks and dried fruit and sweets and chocolates. I was so happy to have received so much from all of my loved ones that I stayed up until 3:00 A.M. writing letters to everyone. I'll never forget that as I was writing to my sweet wife, about 10:40, the Budapest station was transmitting a violin rendition of the song "Although you're far away …" I was overwhelmed with emotion.

January 5, 1941

On Sunday again I sent a card to my wife with Tosonides and 500 dr. with Theodoridies. Later on that night my blankets got totally soaked from the rain that was coming through a hole in our tent. I got rid of the wet blanket, found a heavy piece of tent material and covered up, thus escaping the pouring rain. I imagine my sweet wife sitting and listening to the news tonight. Perhaps our thoughts met at the moment that the news was interrupted ...

We've stayed in this location for almost a month. Most probably we will be ordered to move again, since our troops have already advanced ahead. We have no animals and I wonder how we will be able to transfer all of our supplies.

January 6, 1941

The cards rained in again tonight: four from my wife and one from my sister Popi. She tells me—very indirectly though—that something is wrong with my sister Sofia, who is in Athens with my mother. I am really concerned about Sofia. I don't know how to help from here. I don't know how her illness is going to develop. I will ask Mr. Kastanakis for help. It will really cost me a lot if something happens to her. Tomorrow I will send a letter to Popi, my father and my Chrysoula. From now on I will send 500 dr. to Sofia monthly.

January 8, 1941

The morning brought an almost summer-like day and it smells of spring. We continue to stay in the same position. Early on, our troops began the attack against the height past 1220 location. Our artillery started to fire, using the shells that had been carried up with extreme difficulty by our guys and our animals. Unfortunately, few of our animals remain because of the extreme cold and the lack of good food.

Although the Italians have been kicked out of many places, the successes of our army have not been satisfactory. Despite all that, today all the officers received a laudatory telegram from General Demaratos commending them for a job well done.

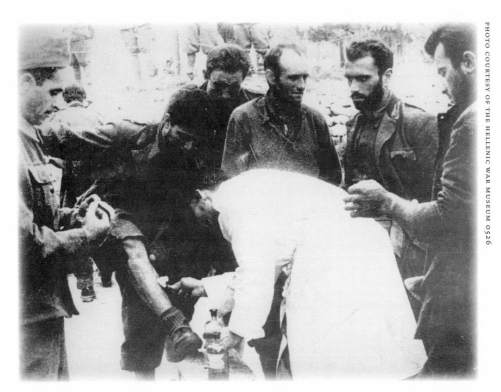

Tending the wounded.

For me it was a super restful day. After my usual letter writing and sending, I did my patient rounds; then I went to the kitchen to arrange the mess. This job provides such a happy and creative diversion for me! From the meat supplies that were brought up for our unit, I had put aside the livers and kidneys and instructed the cook to fix them with onions and vinegar *"stifatho"*[24] specially for the officers. He was complaining that he did not have any butter, but olive oil was a fabulous substitute. I instructed him to add some garlic that I gave him (from my very own supply—which I guard like my eyeballs). He kept some very special pieces for me, so I could be the official taster. I have to admit that they were divine even though cold! The cook also made a pretty good bean soup. After stuffing

---

24 A Greek stew.

myself with two mess pots of bean soup, enhanced with some extra olive oil and garlic, I had to save a third pot for tomorrow.

At around 1:00 P.M. I tried to rest on my bed; however, the Italian airplanes started bombing. There were very many. Somehow they always seem to be bombing when their forces are retreating, and they get no results. Perhaps they came because the weather was good and they wanted to annoy us.

Anyway, it finally quieted down and I was falling asleep, when my silly hostler, Sideris (whom I had given permission to go to Kakosi to buy some meat for himself, with specific instructions to be back by 3:00 P.M.) woke me up. It was now 6:00 P.M. He had some sort of lame excuse for being late and he wanted to make sure I was not too mad.

Well, he succeeded in disturbing me, but in any case, today was the most restful day since the beginning of the war.

Oh, I forgot to mention that after lunch I smoked my 9th cigarette.

January 10, 1941

Today, like the previous two, is filled with food, drink and rest. Last night something amazing happened: I received a package with two *vasilopites* from my wife and I shared one with those who were present. Incredibly, in the last piece, which was destined for me, the knife cut into the coin that my sweetheart had put in the pita as it is the custom. The coin fell upon my piece, perhaps a good omen ...

I sent 1,000 dr. to my mother and cards to my Chrysoula and Mahi. I also received a very delayed (Nov. 28) letter from my father-in-law.

Last night my friend Tosonides and I talked about Thessaloniki, some of the events there and some of our lives there. Home, for us, is not just the bricks and stones, the faces and souls of those we love; it's not just the collective moments that we lived there, or the places that we were accustomed to; home for us is who we have become and who we are, and this feeling of nostalgia is like a magnetic or gravitational force pulling our beings to their correct resting places. We can identify with Odysseus' nostalgia, his search for Home, for himself. Perhaps all men and all beings have this homing instinct, but for the Hellen [Greek] it is a racial trademark more than the color of our skin.

Such sweet nostalgic moments, our memories and chat transferred us back to our dearest town, and so dreaming we went to bed around 12:00.

In the morning Tosonides left for the supply headquarters. Perhaps he will stay in Sevrani for several days, since the 4th Artillery has already started for Sevrani. I don't think that he will find us in the same camp because we'll move within the week.

January 12, 1941

A joyous surprise again for me last night: I received 23 letters—most from Chrysoula! She also sent me a watercolor painted by her own hands; it will provide my only intellectual and aesthetic nourishment for my deprived psyche. I was up all night again writing to her and to my mother, brother and others.

In the morning I sent 1,000 dr. to my Chrysoula. She will guard it better than I. I have to let them know not to send me anything

PHOTO BY ALEXANDER LINDSAY

A typical postcard of the time.

other than food—which we can eat. Anything else will be extra luggage and hard to move.

We are getting ready to depart. Almost the whole artillery unit has gone; only our squadron remains.

This morning, as I listened to the liturgy, my thoughts flew home to Aunt Mahi, who always plays it on the radio, and all of our friends and their families. Home is all that we dream of, home is why we fight, home is what we are; there is nothing more that can explain this.

Jan. 13, 1941
My dearest Phaedia,

So there are some small joys left! Today I got your cards of Dec. 31st, and Jan. 1st and 2nd and I read them over and over. How I wish you could have written me more things about your life up there, I'm so thirsty for your news. I'm sorry you have not received all the things I sent you for New Year's.

Last night a horrible wind was blowing. Around twelve I went to bed but it was impossible for me to fall asleep, my thoughts were running with you. I could see you asleep under your tent in the snow. I was thinking you might not have enough covers and be cold. It was impossible for me to shut my eyes. Then around 3:00 A.M. someone rang the doorbell; for a second I thought that it might be you, but it was not our signal ring. I went out on the terrace to see who it could possibly be at this hour. They needed you for some medical emergency....

In the past three hours since I went to bed all was covered with snow, but at that moment the sky was clear and the moon brilliantly lit the city. It was a magical sight.

They are right when they say that the January moon is the most brilliant. I stood for a while on the terrace barefoot, in my nightgown, and took in this mystical sight. I thought the world would have been so beautiful had those Italians not started this war that separated so many loved ones and destroyed their ability to share beautiful moments.

I went to my bed and fell asleep, with the picture of the moon before me; who knows, perhaps you are looking at the same moon through some opening in your tent.

I want to write you so much more, my dear Phaedia. I want to write you about my love for you, about our parting, about my pain. I don't forget however that my darling is not too romantic and that he wants me to write to him more practical things. He probably is surprised that his wife remains the sentimental girl he first encountered.

Here is some practical information: You ask me how much money I need for the house every month. I spent the least amount possible. And don't you worry about me. I spend only the absolutely necessary for food and the rest goes to fixing up things in the house.

Write to me as frequently as you can; your letters are my only joy.

I kiss you countless times.

January 14, 1941

After 36 days at this location, yesterday we got an order to leave.

We were supposed to get going at 9:00 A.M., but our animals did not arrive until 11:30 and at about 12:00 they started to move slowly.

Alas, our animals are exhausted. Even without a load, they have difficulty moving, so how can we expect them to move our supplies? I have compassion for them and always think of my best and brave mate Lemargos ...

We had to make some quick decisions. I had Sublieutenant Karasavas with me and all of Tosonides' supplies. The beds, stretchers and blankets had to be loaded; all other boxes, including what was most valuable to me—my wife's letters and things she made for me—had to remain at the camp site. I also had to leave my nurses and my medical supplies. And, we had to leave our tent and all our little special places that we had gotten used to in the past month.

We knew this was coming, but little did we know or imagine the wretched hardship and suffering that was to follow.

Heavily loaded pack animals.

We started our walk towards Zaberzani [Zaberzan]. We marched immersed in mud for at least three hours, until we arrived at the river that we had to cross. I have to note that none of the officers accepted a horse for himself, none except for the general. We had to cross the river barefoot. By the time I got there, many of our troops had already crossed it. I took off my boots, socks and even long underwear and got into the freezing water. It came up to my knees and I had to walk for twenty meters or so. When I got to the opposite shore I could not stand on my feet. I rubbed them quickly with alcohol and dried them. My nails hurt for the rest of the march, which lasted for many more hours. At the same time, we had to take care of all the loads that kept falling off the animals. Finally, after a huge struggle and effort and after passing through the village Mogenska [Muzhencke], we arrived in Zaberzani. I found my commander in a house, where I laid my bedding and, after eating a piece of cheese and halvah, I went to bed and luckily slept well.

I forgot to write that along the way I ran across two dead Greek soldiers who unfortunately had been abandoned ... not a pretty sight. I tried not to look but the corner of my eye caught their faces.

One had open eyes, almost staring at me; the other had a gaping mouth and the water of the creek that he had fallen in was running through it. Their open eyes, the gaping mouth and the water haunted me; with every step I took the rhythmic sound of the running water and sight of the open eyes and mouth came back like a tune of a song that sticks in your head for hours. I wished we could have stopped and buried them, burial brings closure, but we could not afford such luxuries of decency. What could I even have been thinking of, we were at war and on the move ... on the move so as not to meet the same fate, I didn't want to be fatalistic, I wanted to believe in some salvation for martyrs; these abandoned Greek soldiers were martyrs to me. Here was my forgotten religious upbringing shining through, and I have to admit that I found solace in that thought.

Our lieutenant, Christopoulos, was moved to Savas' unit and I sent Anagnostou to the hospital with acute tonsillitis.

Now everything is icy but, happily, we are under a roof. Outside, this minute, it is snowing very heavily. Today—now—we are going to eat dry food: meat, halvah, cheese. I'm worried about my things and my medical supplies. My only consolation is that I might receive a letter. Late this morning, outside the Albanian house where we are staying, I found a coin, Greek, perhaps King George I. It appears that I am very lucky.

January 15, 1941

Around 1:30 A.M. the messenger came with new orders. We have to take some new position—Tsepani [Cepan]—in order to back up and sustain our infantry attack. We are absolutely at a dead end with respect to the horses. We can move only in small sections at a time. It looks like we will start the march again. There are, however, many rumors that our squadron will retire for rest after the capture of Veration [Berat].

I personally am sick and tired of this whole expedition. I'm homesick beyond description; I'm nostalgic for my wife, my bed, my home and all.

Today, after such a long stay in the first Albanian village—Skoro-

Dr. Electris (center) in Zaberzani with his nurses and Albanian hosts.

vod—I drank a large glass of fresh milk. The landlord did not want any money, so I gave him some of my halvah. How can a drink of milk become so coveted? Am I becoming bizarre? Well, I just don't care, I'd love to have some more milk again. We'll see.

With all this commotion, it's been almost three days since I've written to my wife. For sure I will write two cards tonight and send one with the 11th Division and one with the 15th Division to increase the chances of her getting one. With all this movement I'm worried about how all my supplies are going to find me. We are supposed to go to Tsepani, but tonight for certain we will stay in Zaberzani.

It has been four hours since the general and all the officers left Zaberzani. Karasavas and I have stayed behind because he is running a very high fever. At this moment it is 38.5°C. He is in no condition to move.

Finally this afternoon my two nurses arrived from our old camp 1037. I could not believe it, but these two gentlemen left all the supplies and one of the other nurses behind to guard them. How do they think all these supplies are going to move? Now I have to send those thoughtless men back with a couple of the poor animals, for which I have more compassion, to fetch the stuff.

January 16, 1941
When our commander left he was planning to return in the evening of the 16th. Instead he gave an order; he ordered everyone to go to Tsepani except for me and Karasavas, who were to remain in the old house of the Albanian. Around 5:00 P.M. Tosonides, not knowing of the new orders, came looking for the general. Then he decided to spend the night with us in the Albanian's house.

January 17, 1941
Yesterday I smoked my 11th cigarette.

I woke up in a good mood, though I had dreamed of people I did not want to dream of; they were all grieving about their unfortunate circumstances, and I was sort of bandaged and useless to them, unable to come to their aid. Some faces were of patients and some of family and friends, continuously transforming like moving clouds and taking on new parts, until I awoke. Perhaps it was too warm; it was the first time since the war started that I slept without long underwear and socks. It should have been a more restful sleep. Somehow this dream reinforced the reality of this existing and persisting wartime expedition. My dreams in life are of healing my patients and of building my nest, but these dreams are being deferred again. I hope that they're only temporarily deferred.

I really hope that with all these diversions (small ones like looking for food and a warm place to stay, and the big ones like taking care of the wounded and getting rid of this crazy enemy), I do not lose my commitment to my aspirations. I have to stay closely connected to my goals and keep seeing them with my mind's eye because I don't want them to slip away from me; I don't want to end up dead on one of the mountainsides, I have no need for martyrdom.

Around 10:00 A.M., some injured soldiers arrived. One of them was injured very seriously with a bullet in his upper left arm. Although I did not have my supplies, I managed to take care of him quite sufficiently. The injury was extensive and serious. Meanwhile Karasavas continues with the high temperature. Yesterday I gave him a one-gram shot of quinine.

Fortunately, we will stay in the old Albanian house for today as well.

It is now 7:30 P.M. I spent all afternoon with that very seriously injured soldier. I asked him a lot of questions as I was bandaging him. It looked like his injury was self-inflicted. His name is Savvas Kazakas, and when they found him he was not at battle but alone in a stable. This war is testing people's nerves and sanity. Tomorrow someone else will have to look into the situation.

For the past two days it has been raining and this morning, after a hailstorm, it has started to snow. The snow has blanketed everything, covering and beautifying the embattled landscape. It looks soft and clean. Yesterday I sent a card, but I have received no mail.

January 18, 1941

I sent a note from the general to Nikolaides, who is still in Kakos. The general explained that the injured, Karasavas and I were to remain in the Albanian's house with all the supplies. All the other officers, with their beds and blankets, were to join the general. So for a while, at least, we will remain in this village until we receive further orders.

It is said, and is a fact, that our soldiers have advanced very far and the destination of the XVth Unit is the city of Veration. After that, the XVth will be replaced by another unit and, together with the XVth, our squadron will be relieved as well. Let's hope that this is going to happen soon enough.

Dr. Electris (far right) with the family of his Albanian host in Tsepani.

I complained to my Albanian landlord that he is not taking good care of us and we might have to look for another place to stay. He was really worried. By having us stay at his place he is well immune from soldiers raiding and looting his house. So for lunch he tried to impress us by cooking us fried steaks and potatoes. For the first time in two and a half months I had a home-cooked meal. It was not anything gourmet, but it was not bad at all. I also sent Sideris to get some supplies and in two days I will send Karasavas' hostler to get more.

Our unit has arrived in Prishte. Here it is still snowing, and there is nearly 30 cm of snow on the ground. I wish I had my camera. I could have taken some great photographs.

I hadn't finished these lines when I heard people calling me from outside. Finally all our things have arrived from Kakosi. I offered cigarettes to everyone and treated them to whatever food I had.

My nurse said that he received three packages for me, which he gave to Officer Nikolaides, and they would not be here until tomorrow.

I went back to my writing, and as I was about to stop, (around 6:00 P.M.) the rest of the officers and Nikolaides arrived. I received everyone in our room and opened the packages that contained chocolates and my camera and film and gloves fragrant with my sweet wife's essence. My mother's package had two pairs of socks, a scarf, raisins and figs. I treated everyone to the goodies. I am totally satisfied. I will write letters and send them tomorrow.

January 20, 1941

Yesterday we stayed almost alone in the Albanian's house in a room that I must describe. It was a corner room that faces south. It had windows with window seats on each side. It had a fireplace that was not being used—a stove was taking its place. The stove was the first of its kind I have seen in a house. It was made of some special kind of metal and it appeared to be a luxury item. The ceiling of the room was beautifully decorated. In the middle there was a big circle and in its center was a painted, gilded head surrounded with rays. The ceiling was walnut with square designs and the Pythagorean emblem was carved in each corner. The molding around the ceiling had painted birds. The furniture consisted of a buffet, a small built-in cabinet, two chairs made of deerskin and a small round table. It was considered one of the most formal rooms.

The landlord treated us well; we had milk for my patient and red bean soup, fresh butter and meat for me. It would have been good to stay here a little longer, but orders came for us to move, although Karasavas was not significantly better. I took the opportunity to bathe, the second time since my bath in the village of Skorova. I took a bath and washed my hair in a narrow wooden tub in a storage room. A huge fire, in a fireplace across from me, kept me warm and there was a big bucket of extra water to rinse off. Oh, the pleasure of being clean!

After my bath I prepared all our blankets and remaining supplies. The landlord cooked for us some pilaf with our rice. So we unwillingly ate the so-called *siktir pilaf*[25] made from our own rice. Anyway, after examining a few sick women and giving them some medicine as well as giving some of my sweets to the children, I loaded Karasavas on one horse and the supplies on the other and headed towards Tsepani. I gave a special paper to the landlord certifying that he had been a great host and great help, to protect him from other passing Greek troops.

After an hour of steady climbing on a muddy and very wet path, we arrived in Tsepani without much trouble. We stayed in the first house, where the general and the captain stayed yesterday. The room was small but beautiful, worth a few words of description. It was again a south-facing room with windows and a fireplace. The wooden ceiling had a six-sided star painted in the center, and in each corner there were triangles with painted birds inside.

The first thing the landlord asked me was if I am *zabit*, or *komandand*[26], and when he learned that I was *Doctór* it was magic! Fortunately, my profession has universal appeal; I'm in demand at all times even among the richest and most powerful. I find that most of the time it helps being a generalist; I know more and can do almost anything and everything, although I'm useless when I encounter special injuries like those of the eye or the spine. It also helps me among these poor Albanians. I feel like a semi-god; they must not have seen a doctor in years. I hate to think that I'm so privileged, but I honestly would love to be of some help if they need it.

With great pleasure the landlord opened the room, made us coffee and prepared us pasta for dinner. We gave dinner to Karamoshos as well. It appeared that he was very hungry. We are getting ready for bed. There are rumors that our squadron is coming here, and so I will get some more mail. I don't know what orders I will get, but I'll worry about them later.

---

25 Literally "the devil's rice;" a dish, usually rice, that is fed to unwelcome guests in the hope that they soon would be gone.

26 *Zabit* is Turkish for "soldier." In 1940, Albania had only recently gained its independence from the Ottoman Empire, and many Albanians still used Turkish words. "Komandand" means "commander" in Albanian.

January 21, 1941

Once again I had a restless night. Perhaps the pillow I had made with my clothes was too overstuffed and was not comfortable. Despite all that, I awoke to a fabulous sun-filled day with a sky so clear that it was almost translucent. Such a warm and dry day provided the perfect opportunity to do some wash. Immediately I had Sideris wash all the clothes I wore in Zaberzani. I also had a visit by Sublieutenant Eliades and we lunched on tea, *kouramana* and cheese. I took some pictures, but I am not sure if they will turn out because my camera was not working too well.

For the photos I wore the beige sweater that my wife has made for me. I have a mustache that is beginning to get long enough to be able to turn it. I have gained some weight and I am hardly recognizable. I also had someone take a picture of Sideris and me as he was doing the wash.

"Immediately I had Sideris wash all the clothes I wore in Zaberzani."

For lunch Karasavas and I had a couple of cans of sardines, *kouramana* and halvah. I have to note here that, when there is food available, I'm intentionally overeating and trying to gain some weight because I don't know what will follow; we might end up just like the horses, starved and overworked.

After lunch we were visited by two Albanian men with whom we desperately tried to communicate, but had a very hard time. Finally, using word analysis and putting together all my knowledge of languages, including Latin, I figured out that they needed me to examine a sick relative. I treated them to some cognac, cigarettes and walnuts that our landlord brought us and will deal with them tomorrow. Now I have to go for patient rounds.

January 22, 1941

After my rounds I took some more pictures in front of the village well. It was just outside the house that served as the makeshift hospital. Our dinner at night was some inedible noodles that our landlord (called Asker) offered us. Perhaps we should have eaten them at lunch, because then we wouldn't have had to worry that we would not sleep because of upset stomachs. Happily our hostlers felt sorry for us and prepared us something light to eat. Breakfast was better, with milk and sheep butter. Sergeant Kontos came from headquarters with mail. The letter from my wife had been written on the 30th of December, an answer to my letter written on November 17th. I also received two letters from Nitsa written on the 5th and 6th of January, and she is complaining to me that I don't write to her. I also got letters from my brother George, my sister Evridiki and uncle Theodore. I wish them the best for thinking of me.

Now that I have some time I'm going to answer all of them and then I will go and pay a visit to an old Albanian man who invited me for coffee. It's interesting getting to know some of these people; they are hospitable and friendly. They have different customs than ours, but they are a proud bunch. Some of them are very needy with respect to medical care, and I'll try to aid them the best I can.

Yesterday I smoked my 12th cigarette (Aroma brand).

In Tsepani "outside the house that served as the makeshift hospital ... with our landlord (called Asker)," Karasavas and Karamoshos.

January 23, 1941

I have to discuss food again—I'm sort of preoccupied with food now. Of course I'm always interested in food—one of life's greater joys—but now, because of its absence and because I have more time on my hands, it has become a major preoccupation.

Since last night we have been sampling some typical, local Albanian country cuisine. We had some *lallangites*, a fried sort of puffy pastry sprinkled with sugar. Then we had some kind of a pie consisting of two pieces of dough stuffed with bulgur, an interesting tasty concoction but a bit on the pasty side. After satisfying our appetites we gave the rest to our very happy grooms.

I'm very pleased that I sent my letters with Sergeant Kontos to my wife and others. She was in my dreams last night. How I wish that things were reversed, that my Chrysoula, my home, my neighbors were the reality and this expedition was a bad dream, a nightmare that I could wake up from. Oh boy, I'm so homesick! I can identify with Odysseus ...

Karamoshos came with an order from the general that I should move with my staff and supplies to Nishitse [Nishice] and leave Karasavas and the other patients who were recuperating in Prishte. Meanwhile, the captain who is supposed to be responsible for our move has not sent us horses yet. Perhaps he does not consider medical personnel important or necessary.

I don't know how or when we will arrive in Nishitse. I hope no major emergency occurs meanwhile. The truth is, despite all the sidetracking with the Albanians, I'm pretty sick and tired of staying here. I feel very isolated without my other fellow officers. However, I'm glad that the animals haven't arrived today because it is raining nonstop and cataclysmically. We are using up our supplies and hoping that no additional ones arrive, so we won't have to be hauling them all the way to Nishitse.

January 25, 1941

Yesterday was a monotonous, worrisome day. I spent it trying to figure out how to get out of here. I just don't get what the captain is thinking when he sends the horses to pick up backpacks instead of the sick soldiers and the medical personnel and all of the medical supplies. Almost all of the recovering patients have moved on and we have received no other food supplies; it appears that they have forgotten us. Happily our landlord, Asker, makes some *lallangites* for us every night and we have something to eat. Had I not been taking care of the sick Albanians I would have considered myself completely useless.

The only exciting thing that happened was a huge explosion yesterday afternoon. As it turned out a goat had stepped on an Italian mine and somehow lived to bleat her story afterwards.

In the morning I had decided that I was going to Prishte on my own. So, I packed my blankets and a bed and some major medical supplies and paid a strong young Albanian with the name of

With Tosonides and a patient. "Had I not been taking care of the sick Albanians I would have considered myself completely useless."

In Tsepani, "I packed ... some medical supplies and paid a strong young Albanian with the name of Ohran [center, behind Dr. Electris] to carry them to Prishte."

Dr. Electris and Ohran (left).

Ohran to carry them to Prishte. I packed and prepared the rest of our supplies for movement so they would be ready when I sent for them.

If I could not send horses, Asker was going to find someone else to haul the rest of our supplies and Karasavas would have to walk to Prishte. I had Karasavas' groom, Melissaris, come with me as well. We had pictures taken in front of the house that we had stayed in, with all our hosts. On the way I had another picture taken with Ohran. Ohran was a good guide and he took us through a special mountain path that was not too muddy.

When we arrived in Prishte I realized that it was in a state of real confusion. Things were sort of wild, everyone executing some order that they considered of utmost priority, and there were no horses to be found anywhere. So I sent Ohran and Melissaris back to bring Karasavas and the rest, otherwise, they were going to be left there.

In Prishte I found Tosonides, Karamoshos and Syropoulos with supplies.

There are rumors that as soon as Veration falls we will be sent to Florina or Serres and will be replaced by the artillery divisions of Serres or Crete.

Today I will stay in Prishte; the mail came, but I received nothing.

January 26, 1941

Last night Tosonides and I slept in the building where all the supplies were stored. It rained all night and the rain seeped between the slate tiles on the wrecked roof and splattered my face. The roofs of all the buildings here are made out of slate slabs instead of ceramic tiles. I had to move my bed next to the fireplace and as I was beginning to enjoy the warmth and the sweetest part of my sleep,

PHOTOS BY DR. THEODORE ELECTRIS

In Prishte: Tosonides and his staff with Dr. Electris' nurse Karamoshos (third from left).

" ... we loaded our things on some terrible-looking horses and started off for Nishitse."

Prishte, preparing to depart. From right: Sublieutenant Moshopoulos, Sub-lieutenant Kaloudes, Dr. Electris, Tosonides, Katzurakis, Nurse Karamoshos and Sergeant Nerantzis.

I was awakened again by personnel who tramped in and out while doing the morning resupplying of the troops.

This morning I received a note from the general who said that he is here and would love to see me.

Yesterday I had an orange. At noon I smoked my 17th cigarette. I have to make special note of the rare luxuries such as an orange, and when I get home I will never let one rot or go to waste, even if there are plenty of them around. As far as the cigarettes are concerned, the little bit of nicotine gives me a much-needed lift.

At night I got a package from my mother with two pairs of socks, knit by her golden hands, and five candy bars. My poor mother; I will forever be her little boy!

January 27, 1941

In Prishte we took some pictures again, then we loaded our things on some terrible-looking horses and started off for Nishitse. I have to mention that these horses were sent to us supposedly for carrying medical supplies from the supply headquarters. However, they were not loaded properly and half the supplies fell off a short distance from the headquarters—half-ass jobs!

We left Prishte around 1:00 P.M. and, after a six-hour climb and after passing from Rehovitsa [Rahovice], we arrived in Nishitse.

Along the way I met up with Karasavas, who was now well and had taken a path through the forest. I also finally met up with my nurse, Karamoshos, who was walking by himself and looking for me.

In Nishitse I was a guest in the quarters of the officers of the 4th Artillery. The room here was similar to the supply room where I slept in Prishte, but the roof was not leaking and the fireplace was so immense that a complete tree trunk was burning inside it. I set up my bed and tried to rest. I did not want anything to eat, as I had half a can of sardines along the way. Mr. Noutsos offered me some tea, which I took with great pleasure.

Along the way I met up with the mail carrier and gave him three cards: one for my mother and two for my wife.

January 28, 1941

This afternoon I got a letter from my sweet wife. She writes about our family finances. I see that she is handling business very well. She is very smart and focused. It's such great consolation to me to know that she is well and in good spirits. My poor sweet wife, she is alone with concerns and responsibilities that she never thought she would have to face all by herself. If only she knew how much I owe her for her love.

I also received letters from my brother and sister and my friend Antonis who wrote to me about the death of his brother-in-law. It is unfortunate that Antonis' sister has lost the husband it took her so long to find, and just as they were starting their family.

Here I am so far removed from my world, unable to be supportive and helpful to family and friends. My bizarre reality is looking for horses, figuring out how to cook mess food and treating some poor Albanians.

I'm replying to all the letters; it's the least I can do....

Around five o'clock I got an order to join the artillery unit immediately. As it was a climb of several hours and it was already getting dark, I decided to go very early the next morning.

January 29, 1941

I woke up at around twenty minutes to seven and immediately started tying up and packaging my things. My groom and I loaded our things on our backs, with me carrying my medical supplies and the gun, and started off.

There are no words to describe what we saw along the way. I will never ever forget that one hill. It was as though we were walking through open graves, staring death in the face. The dead, most of them Italian but quite a few Greeks as well, were lying among exploded ammunition and mines, machine guns, and shells. The description of the wounds could fill several volumes of medical journals. There were soldiers with open skulls, torn guts, with bodies riddled with bullets. Even my training as a doctor did not prepare me for such a grisly and catastrophic sight! I observed that many of the dead had no shoes and some no trousers; our soldiers who were short of boots and trousers had taken them from the dead. An overwhelming and oppressive feeling overtook us. Perhaps it was the throbbing awareness of the raw gruesomeness of the war and of imminent danger. Perhaps the air over that hill was laden with the spirits of those dead and, like a heavy fog, was wrapping us in sadness. My thoughts were a poor memorial for those young lives, both Greek and Italian, that had been cut short, wasted, their life dreams and songs petrified within their dead bodies, never to be realized and never to be sung, on these wild impenetrable mountains of Albania—all because of some crazy tyrants or leaders!

When we finally arrived at camp there was no tent for us. Tonight will be the first time in 15 days that I will have camp mess (pilaf and meat). After all I saw I don't think I'll be able to swallow a thing. Karasavas is still in Prishte.

January 30, 1941

As of last night the camp life has started again. I'm sharing a tent with a colleague. I was so mentally and physically exhausted that I slept in the clothes I arrived in. I haven't mailed my letters yet.

January 31, 1941

An unexpected air attack at around 5:30 P.M. shook us up and terrified us. I have to admit that I was really scared, and I could not hide my fear. They were strafing us and bombing us and with my own eyes I saw death coming in the fiery path the bullets left as they rained destruction upon everything they touched. One of the planes was so close, not even 100 meters above us, that I could see the pilot. I had just been resting and thinking of my sweet wife when they came and shook us up. Fifteen minutes later there was another raid that bombed the opposite hillside. Nikolaides and I had taken cover to protect ourselves, but there was no good place to hide and the bullets could find one anywhere. It was a matter of luck and coincidence that we were not hit. Tomorrow we will have to agonize about new situations, especially if the weather remains good.

February 1, 1941

I got mail from my sweet wife and I wrote her two cards. Tomorrow I will send money to my wife and mother. I got my salary of 5,223 dr.

February 3, 1941

We continue to stay at the same camp near the village of Vinan. My tent arrived yesterday and now I have a roof over my head.

Nikolaides and I are sitting under the light of a makeshift oil lamp fashioned from a mess dish, a little oil and a wick made of medical cotton. We made a small brazier and now we are making a feeble attempt to dry out our boots. Everything is wet, saturated with moisture, soaked in mud. Today the airplanes dropped propaganda papers, but I haven't seen one.

Depiction of the battle on the Tepeleni Heights.

February 4, 1941

It's been four days since I've come to this camp and it has not stopped raining. The rain, especially today, is something I've never experienced before. It feels like buckets of water have been falling non-stop for hours on top of my tent. As far as the mud is concerned, I can find no words to describe it: mud, mire, mortar—Hell.

The ground has been churned into a doughy muck by the soldiers' boots and the horses' hoofs and the machinery and artillery wheels; there isn't a single untracked spot in sight. At some places you could sink in mud up to your knees. On this dramatically miserable muddy stage the work and struggle of our poor soldiers is taking place. What effort, what agony and pathos—and how many victims! It will be such a pity if all is wasted.

I have to describe a couple of incidents that took place an hour ago.

Our 13th Infantry Regiment, with the support of our battery unit, had attacked and seized a hill near Bosketto (height near the village of Dodovece). There were many wounded who were being brought to us through the field just across from my tent, where the ground was as I've described it. The stretchers with the wounded were carried by three, and sometimes by two, soldiers instead of the proper four—one for each corner of the stretcher. They struggled to walk through the mud in the pouring rain—slipping, sliding and falling and pushing, with their heads drooping like those in the pictures I have seen of the workers on the Volga River. Sometimes as they walked they would slip and fall and would try to get up. The wounded would be screaming and grabbing onto the stretcher, if they could, with those parts of their body that were not wounded, so they would not fall into the mud. Sometimes all would fall and try to rise again, lifting the stretcher that was stuck and sucked by the mud.

At one point, I saw two guys trying to carry a stretcher with a wounded man who was screaming loudly. The carrier in the back of the stretcher was crying and his face was sheet white. He could not carry the stretcher because his hands were slipping; he would set the stretcher down and try to pick it up again. The carrier in the front would scream and swear at him and the wounded man would cry, beg and try to hold onto the stretcher to keep from sliding backwards into the muddy hell below. Suddenly the carrier in the front dropped the stretcher, and both the wounded man and the stretcher splashed into the mud. This particular carrier then staggered towards the carrier in the back, who was crying as he was trying to get up. With his fist, he hit him very hard in the face. In fact he hit him so hard that the poor guy fell backwards in the mud, was knocked out and was not moving. For a second the guy that did the hitting was scared, thinking that he had killed the other carrier; he bent over and grabbed him by the neck and started shaking him. When he saw that he was moving, he started swearing and cursing him again. The fallen carrier crept up out of the mud, continuously crying and ignoring the other one who was screaming. He started walking away from the whole scene as if in a daze. Meanwhile the wounded man was lying in the mud and rain, crying ... What could the poor carrier have done under all these conditions? It was hard for the horses to walk through the field; how could an overloaded man, with wet slippery hands, be expected to walk through it? These conditions are so undignified, humiliating, inhumane! Perhaps he was the one who sent six other carriers, who soon arrived and lifted the wounded man out of the mud.

Meanwhile, under these wretched conditions of mud and rain, the battle is raging. We are very busy taking care of the wounded, who are arriving nonstop with every imaginable trauma caused by artillery shell fragments, machine gun fire, but mostly mortars. Our poor soldiers patiently take their turns, silently, not protesting the fact that we cannot work any faster; some of them are even trying to help others ... and we, we the medics, try to do the best we can in primitive conditions, lacking both tools and, I dare to admit, expertise in trauma surgery. I was never trained to do trauma surgery under such great pressure and in such primitive conditions. I have no time to think of alternatives; sometimes I barely have time to disinfect one trauma before I must deal with another more severe one.

In the background as I hear the explosions of the guns and the mines, I think of the parents, wives and children of our men,

The proper way to carry a stretcher.

who are agonizing about them without really knowing how great the dangers are—even the natural dangers of this wild and rugged terrain—and tears come to my eyes. I feel for every soldier whose family is waiting at home for him, like my family, my sweet wife, my beloved relatives and friends, and I wish with all my body and soul for this war to end. It is an unfair, unjust war that we were dragged into, and it is going to fill the whole world with bitterness and pain. Will our poor nation be a nation of widows, orphans and lame men?

I send money and cards to Chrysoula, Mother and Sofia. Because we have been moving we haven't received mail yet. Oh, how I need the morale boost and the psychological high that a note from a loved one brings!

February 6, 1941

Since last night I have again had the wireless in my tent, and life here will take on the same routine and grind as the life at the camp in Kakosi.

PHOTOS COURTESY OF THE HELLENIC WAR MUSEUM—0580 (TOP), 0166 (LOWER LEFT), 0066 (LOWER RIGHT)

Transporting the wounded.

The general and the captain of our battery remain sick. Today the general's temperature is down, but the captain's intestinal problems continue because I can't stop him from eating—he is such a greedy man!

I sent mail with both the 11th and 15th army divisions but have gotten none, and boy, I could use the lift from some letters.

Feb. 9, 1941
My Darling,
   Today, the 9th of February, is an unforgettable day for me; it is the day I came into this world and the day that I met you. Remember, two years ago, a light-filled ballroom ... music ... evening gowns ... dancing.
   You were seated at a table with some other lady as I approached (an unknown girl to you) to sell some raffle tickets; Then a proposal, followed by a denial, followed by an introduction, then a dance, followed by another dance ... the last of the evening. A question as we danced was followed by a negative answer, and then the statement "perhaps luck will help." I thought then, "Well, somehow, the fragile golden thread that joined our two tables for two hours was going to be broken, like the Mardi Gras streamers that filled the room ..."

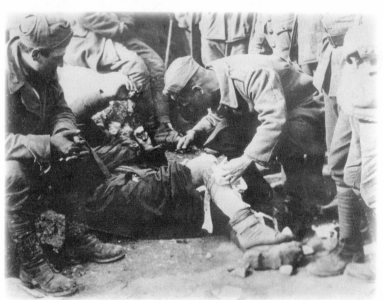

PHOTO COURTESY OF THE HELLENIC WAR MUSEUM—0160

Tending the wounded.

Two years have passed since, and this evening all is so vivid in my mind, that I think it happened yesterday. Luck (but perhaps we helped a little) joined us forever. Little did I know then you would become my most adored one and that I would love you more than my own life.

Phaedia, my only love, the tempest that has parted us will not last long. The sun will shine brilliantly. After the rough seas we will feel joy and peaceful calm.

I know that you will return healthy because I pray with faith for you and your love will protect me as well and we will continue our dreamed life.

It is night; I write to you seated next to the fire with Frifris as my companion. After I finish your letter I will listen to Churchill who will speak from London. Then I will go to bed hoping that in my dream I will find myself in the warm ballroom, dancing with you. I will feel again your soft breath caressing my hair, I will hear you whispering so many things and see that smile that I love so much. Then, tired from the warmth and dizzy from the whirls, I will lean on your shoulder with confidence and all will be as beautiful as it was two years ago tonight.

I kiss you many many times and I wish you sweet dreams.

February 10, 1941

Yesterday noon we moved from our camp near Kiafe Mourit[27] to a new camp near Spandarit.[28] It's the best camp so far with respect to the location and placement of our tents. My tent is set parallel to a creek with running water. Yesterday, after the work of the move, I was able to wash my feet in lots of fresh water. Happily, we also had plenty of sunshine yesterday which helped warm us up and kill some of our body lice.

The better weather has changed our soldiers' mood and increased their appetite for war. The Italian lines are about 1,500 m

---

27 Mountain north of Nishitse.
28 Mountain sight between Spathar and Nishitse.

from our lines, and these days we are expecting that we'll soon start a general attack. A tremendous amount of ammunition has been stockpiled, more than the usual. It is very important for this general attack to be successful. The only bad thing is that our soldiers are malnourished, but this will pass when the roads reopen after we attack. There is a rumor that our units will be replaced after the fall of Veration.

Yesterday we had two accidental hand grenade injuries. Two soldiers were trying to disarm a hand grenade and turn it into an ashtray when it exploded. How stupid!

Today I will take some pictures beside the cannons.

February 12, 1941

As of noon yesterday we started packing again and are on the move, leaving Spandarit. I was disappointed to leave the creek, but war is not a picnic. It was so nice over there and I could wash every morning, but most important the horizon was very open and we could see the enemy planes and had the opportunity to take cover, while in Kiafe Mourit we could never anticipate them, because they could come from every direction. Just before we were ready to depart, a bomber came by. One of the bombs fell about 100 m from our tent. The truth was that I got very scared.

The sun above made our walk towards our new camp feel not too exhausting, although there was enough snow and mud to make the trekking difficult. We walked about 3 km back towards the road to Nishitse and took a new position southwest towards Bosketto.

Amidst all this suffering, hardship and fear, I have to look for every little source of joy, be it a colored cloud, a flower or even the melting snow. I soak up its beauty like a sponge and quench my thirsty spirit and revive my psyche. So, if I'm suddenly killed by an Italian bomb, I won't regret that I haven't noticed those most minute details that make life worth living on this earth. As a matter of fact, I take extra effort to find and celebrate beauty in insignificant things, so they in turn will not regret that they passed unnoticed by me, that I left this earth without appreciating their existence.

The commander's tent and my tent are at a site that has a special charm. It is along the side of a ravine, and the melting snow is creating a tiny creek. One side of the ravine is wooded, with beautiful oak trees and bushes. The woods, however, have recently been significantly thinned down by previous army troops. On the other side of the ravine is a chartreuse meadow with purple blooming crocuses. On this flower-covered mountainside spring is blooming, revealing itself like a young woman undressing in the sun, but on our side, just five meters from the tents, the snow-covered bushes and ground remind us that winter still has us in its grip.

This is indeed a magical place, and just this morning at dawn, I could hear a nightingale sing as other birds accompanied it. It feels as if the spring is really here, because it starts to warm up from the sun around 10 o'clock and stays warm until sunset. The moon rises from our side of mountain, and from our tents it appears to come right out of the mountaintop as it moves through the trees. Perhaps I would not have happened upon such a sight if it were not for this war. Despite all this natural beauty, the hardships and exhaustion

In Kiafe Mourit, with nurses Karamoshos, Syropoulos, Sariyiannis, Ekonomou, Sideris and Hondros (who is wearing his shirt for pants because all his other clothes were wet).

are wearing me down and are making it difficult to enjoy anything. When I awoke this morning my whole body was aching.

I sent those first spring crocuses to my love with a letter and wrote cards to my mother and sisters. I'll send them with a soldier who is going to the headquarters. I'm hoping for a letter from my wife.

February 13, 1941

At midnight the horrible explosions of cannons and guns and the terrible sounds of machine guns and grenades started again. The sky is on fire and in all directions the horizon is lit up from the explosions. I try to calm myself down by thinking that they are beautiful and phantasmagoric like fireworks. Alas, it's a delusion, and as the Italians attack the opposite side there will be so many dead and wounded. It's hard to have the stomach for this.

It seems that the Italian attack has failed and our attack is now commencing, starting from Klissoura and extending through the whole area across the enemy lines all the way to Tria Avga.[29] We don't know the results yet, but we're hoping that we have captured the objectives. This morning, simultaneous with our ground attack, our air force started bombing the enemy towards Tria Avga.

I've sent the letters to my wife and have written cards to Nikos and my best man. I haven't answered my sister Sofia, as I'm trying to figure out some way I can help her from far away. I'm not happy with the situation that she is in.

The weather has shown signs of change. Since noon a frigid wind has been blowing, penetrating us to the bone, letting us know that we are going to have another blast of winter.

---

29 "Tria Avga," or "Tre Cukat" in Albanian, is a location marked by three mountain peaks outside Corovode.

Dr. Electris examines a patient across from Tria Avga.

February 15, 1941

The blowing wind lasted for a day and it rained nonstop from morning to night. Now the clouds seem to be dissipating, and there is a strange calm. I've gotten my mail ready to send. I have torn up all the letters that I have received—all except my wife's and some of my mother's and a couple from some friends.

February 17, 1941

Sunday came and went with the monotonous daily routines taking a toll in a different war, the war of nerves. I spent some time dealing with correspondence; I wrote a letter to my commander asking him to make a request to the ministry of health for a free admission to a hospital for my sister Sofia, since I could not help her because I was away at war. I'm certain that my commander will make the appropriate introduction after receiving my letter. I will send a copy of this letter to my sister Evridiki. Sofia's situation concerns me very much; I think about her all the time and I don't have the resources to help her.

I have smoked my 16th cigarette.

The chances are that we will stay at this camp for a while. Today I will write to my Chrysoula.

February 19, 1941

The nonstop rain started again last night. It has stopped everything—even the war. I didn't even move from my bed until two in the afternoon. I can't describe the torrents of water that were coming down the mountain. The water was flooding my tent as well, but the good thing was that, sitting on my bed, I could stay dry. The winter won't loosen its grip. In any case, I have to get up and present myself to our commander.

Yesterday I sent a card to Chrysoula and a letter to Evridiki telling her about the two application letters I sent to the headquarters for my sister Sofia. One of the requests will be forwarded to the city government of Athens and the other to the director of the Health Ministry, Mr. Karabetso, to whom I already sent a personal recommendation letter from my commander.

Today I smoked my 17th cigarette.

February 20, 1941

I smoked my 18th cigarette

I got a letter from my wife. This time, she is happy that she has received my letters. She wants a letter every day. Since I love her so much I can never refuse her wishes!

Feb.21, 1941
My Darling,

These days the hyacinths we have planted in the big pot are all in bloom and I brought them into the living room. Their fragrance perfumes the entire house. The sun comes through the open windows and fills with joyful light all our beautiful furniture. Only the paper that is covering the windowpanes reveals that we are at war.

Early this morning our cat Frifris woke me as he jumped on the bed-stand and made some noise. For a second I thought it was you trying to turn off the alarm clock. Then I felt his warm breath on my face and I got up. Frifris follows me everywhere and never leaves me alone. It is as if he is asking for the extra affection that he used to get from you; I never disappoint him.

The business of accounts receivable is getting slower. People are at the front or somehow have vanished to the countryside. I can manage without all the money and all the asking.

Enclosed is my brother Nikos' address at the front, as well as that of Demetrios Layias. All our friends have received your letters and they send you love. Let me know if you receive all the magazines I send you; I can't imagine that they are extra baggage. Don't get angry with me my love.

I kiss you countless times.
Yours always.

February 22, 1941

It's 11:10 A.M. and I have just returned from my commander's tent. He has been running a temperature for the past two days, and he continues to not feel well; one moment it's his ear, the next his eye, then his ribs that bother him; he just needs special attention. He has gotten used to my rubs and wants them every night; in addition, I have to make his bed and cover him up in a special way.

Aside from being his doctor I also have become his personal chambermaid. That's the army for you.

Outside it's hailing, thundering, lightning, snowing—all of winter's machinations. Like the enemy, it doesn't want to retreat and won't. General Demaratos is visiting us again today. I got letters from some friends and my wife. My sweet wife, how much she cares for me. She hopes that through some miracle I will be returned to her soon; but alas, Tepeleni hasn't fallen and neither have Tria Avga or Veration.

I learned that my colleague Sites and I have been recommended to receive honors for our exceptional services. Some other people were recommended as well, which surprised me because they didn't impress me as doing any extra service. All of these honors and nonsense have no significance to me. What do I care about my advancement in the army? I have no need to be a hero; I'm not an army person and can't get into the military mentality, but that's another story. I'd rather be a simple soldier and have all these military operations end with the ousting and driving out of these damn Italians.

February 25, 1941

That horrible, persistent rain that's torturing us with its slow rot hasn't stopped pouring on us for two days again. I had decided to go to Nishitse to examine the sick and wounded there. Yesterday morning I wanted to leave very early, but it seemed like the rain wanted to spite me—by 6:00 A.M. it was pouring harder and, in addition, the fog was so thick that I could not even see my feet. Finally, around 9:00 A.M., there was a glimpse of the sun and I decided to start off, accompanied by my groom Sideris. We took the path to the right towards the antiaircraft unit and climbed to the mountaintop. The fog had lifted and we could see almost all of Albania—its mountaintops, that is. We could see the enemy lines stretching from Bosketto-Priezi almost up to Tria Avga. After climbing down for an hour and a half, we arrived in the ravine that was our destination.

Immediately and without taking a rest I did my patient rounds and examined all the sick and wounded of the 3rd Unit. Then I went to look for my friends Nikolaides and Tosonides. I was in time for mess—bean soup, which I ate with great appetite. Later I looked for some of my officer friends and took many pictures. After that I examined all the patients of the 4th Unit and, when I finished, we immediately started back towards our camp. On the way we met my nurses, whom I had sent to Trebiska [Trebicke] for medical supplies. Luckily, all of us got back to our camp before it started raining again, which it did as soon as we arrived. The same damn rain!

I could have stayed in Nishitse but I did not accept my fellow officers' invitations because I was worried about lice. I admit that I will miss their company.

When I arrived back at camp I was quite tired, but I had a pleasant surprise in my tent: two physician colleagues of mine. Oh the joys of company, they were my old *parea*. We had such unforgettable times, with joking, laughing, eating and drinking, picnicking and mountain climbing, sharing secrets and confidences—there was such joy and security in our friendship. Our bonds helped us survive medical school and the difficult days of being a refugee. Their visit was just like opening a coveted bottle of wine. We dined together on pilaf and canned food—the mess supper.

I received no mail; in any case, I was too tired to write.

Today I started moving from my bed around 12:00 P.M., because of that stupid rain. We will rot or float away. This weather is causing desperation beyond belief, as if we needed one more thing to oppress us. We have to keep up the hope, though, that spring is not too far off, and that at least one thing, the weather, will change for the better.

Oh please, may the mailman lift my spirits!

February 27, 1941

My wife's letter of February 2nd filled me with emotion. She was reminiscing about our first meetings and how we fell in love, all those beautiful, lively, detailed moments that I so long to relive. How sensitive is my sweet Chrysoula and how I love her!

Now it's raining and snowing at the same time. We have literally rotted! I'm sick and tired of this weather grind. Thank God for the letters; I can forget myself as I float away in the rain. I've been writing since noon and it's now 5 P.M.

Feb. 27, 1941

My dearest Phaedia,

For your name day I wish you many many happy and healthy returns. I hope you get my letter the day of your name day. I hoped that this day would be very different; our house full of flowers in the spring sun, celebrating your first name day with me.

Tomorrow it will be four whole months since you left, four endless months. When each month begins I hope it will be the last month we will be apart—and so time flies in the midst of moments of tears and boredom and consolation and hope.

I'm sure that this day of your name day you will long more for home. You will remember that last year, when you still celebrated it as a single man, perhaps you will remember what you have written in your medical diary.

My Phaedia, if you were near me, I would have never told you that I thought of you in the same way you thought of me, because I did not want to confess to you and not even to myself that you were my one and only love.

[A note at the bottom of the diary's page for this date reads:]

Note: My golden sweet little wife, how much I love her.
—T. E, Feb. 27, 1941

Chrysoula sent Dr. Electris this letter in honor of his name day (March 8). See color version on page 224.

February 28, 1941

It's been four months now since the day I was mobilized, four whole months away from a happiness that I thought I had found but didn't even have a chance to feel. Oh, how many dreams did I weave about the life I would lead with my wife, my medical practice, our future. All was extinguished with just one order: mobilization.

One should not dream of happiness. I'm the least lucky of all. For so many years I searched for my soul mate, always envious of other couples, always feeling sad for being alone. When finally luck gave me a chance, after so many trials and tribulations, and I found my sweet ethereal angel, my Chrysoula, and was settling in to my practice, suddenly all was taken away. My happiness was just beginning. I was just starting to build the foundations of my being, beginning to complete my temple and to see it whole, having the satisfaction of giving happiness to my sweet wife and to those who mattered to me.

Oh, how I wish that the strongest force in the universe will give me the necessary energy and the required power to withstand these extremely unfavorable conditions and circumstances, the power to protect my life, the power to survive. I must survive to realize my dreams, to create my happiness and that of the sweetest angel, my wife. I'm certain that I'm in a position to chase away all that is threatening my goals that are so simple and humble, the goals of a common man. I must and will survive, since my soul mate is waiting for me to give me the happiness I long for with such deep yearning. I'm thankful for this inner journey that brought me to this awareness, this restatement and clarification of my credo. It is now fueling my fire and my power to endure. Somehow this war makes me see more clearly what I want out of life.

March 3, 1941

A surprise yesterday!

Masqueraders arrived from the neighboring unit of Katseri. Along with them there was a bear trainer. He was a tall black man wearing a fez, holding a *san-*

touri.[30] His bear was huge and had bells around its neck. He was followed by an entourage of street women and gypsies. We had quite a few laughs and I took a few pictures. It's good that our guys are in good humor! Well, how could they not be—after two weeks of continuous rain, the sun finally made an appearance to warm our hearts and spirits! I received a card from Chrysoula.

March 6, 1941

Two more days of rain and wind and a glimpse of sun; and today the weather started bouncing between sun and rain. Now we are being visited by two or three enemy planes strafing us with 150 mm shells. The incoming rounds shook us out of the lethargy of the past few days and made us come to our senses. The missiles created deep craters at least five steps wide and hurled dirt and rocks at least 60 m—some landed about 20 m from our tent!

Today I sent to Chrysoula a certificate stating that I'm serving in our unit. This will enable her, if necessary, to leave for Athens or Chalkidiki.

I wrote to my father-in-law to secure passage for everyone in the family. I want him to be able to secure it. I'm worried again. Alas, if war breaks out with Germany, then Thessaloniki will literally become a bloody battlefield.

March 7, 1941
Yesterday afternoon I received your letters.

Thank you for the beautiful flowers; I will hide them together with the few jasmine blossoms I have kept to bring me luck, so that you will return soon. I'm happy your new campsite is so idyllic. Perhaps all of you men will become a little more romantic. Still I worry so about the raids.

Starting very early this morning my first job was to search for the medications you have asked me to send you. I searched your office, all your desk drawers, your medicine cabinets, your medical

---

30 A form of tambourine.

equipment cabinets ... Some time ago I had searched through your desk drawers, as you had specifically instructed me, looking for contracts and billing information, so my dear, inadvertently, I learned some of your secrets ... Don't blame me, blame el Duce.

Anyway, out of all the things that you asked for, I only found ten, as listed below ...

Tomorrow I will try to find the rest at the pharmacist's and at the pharmaceutical company. I don't know if you will be happy, but I have not found any of the other drugs you have requested. I took all the boxes out, read each one individually, and then took out the ones you needed. Do not worry, I will do my best to find what you need.

Meanwhile I have continued the very slow bill collecting, I have to be quite delicate because people have no money, and even if they had it they are nervous about paying their debts back and letting it go; nobody knows what tomorrow will bring.

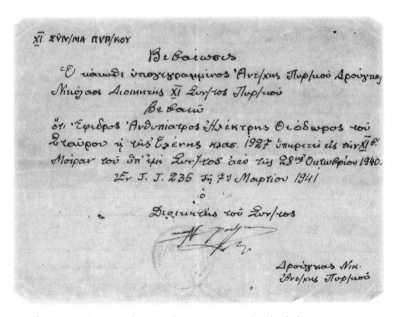

Certificate signed on March 7, 1941, by Lieutenant-Colonel Nikolas Drungas, attesting that Dr. Theodore Electris served as an assistant surgeon in Artillery Unit XI starting October 28, 1940.

Flowers sent by Dr. Electris to Chrysoula that she saved.

> *Do you know what I have found out since the time you left and I got involved in all your business affairs? I learned that the world is much more different than I had imagined it and life has more thorns than roses. So be it, I cannot do anything about it. So long as I have your love I have become strong and have even great courage now that you are away from me.*

March 8, 1941

All day today we've been sitting in the foxholes. An enervation is taking hold. It's now a war of nerves. Four shells fell on our unit and camp. It will be awful if they shell us at night; we won't be able to shut our eyes even for a second.

March 9, 1941

Yesterday my little wife was celebrating my name day. I can only imagine how many people visited her and called her with good wishes for me. Meanwhile I had the great pleasure of receiving a small package (600 g) with envelopes, small oil lamps, a few candies and socks and some drugs that I had requested. How sweet she is and how much she cares for me!

While at camp 1037 we were so heavily and continuously bombed by the Italian heavy artillery that our lives were in constant danger. So our commander, together with an officer and a noncommissioned officer, decided to look for another camping site. I took advantage of the opportunity and went along for the walk. We started around 8:00 in the morning and walked for several hours, returning at around 2:00 in the afternoon. I was sorry that I had not brought my camera. We descended about 200 m and discovered the greenest valley full of blooming cornel-bushes[31] and a loudly rolling creek, not too deep, about one meter wide but crystal clear. So clear that I could not resist bending over to have a drink. In a few spots waterfalls formed, and the surrounding rocks looked like chartreuse velvet gleaming in the sun. There were violets everywhere, and my commander cut one for me to send to my sweetheart. I also chose for her the most beautiful golden flower—it looked like a lily or crocus. I had already sent her a violet one.

We rested and enjoyed nature for a bit, forgetting the menacing conditions we were in, letting Life and the joy of being alive take hold of us ... For a brief moment the world stood still, the rolling creek silenced the guns and we were transported back to a time before man destroyed the innocence of this green valley. What a magical, reinvigorating experience. When life and death are but a hair apart, one has to inhale each good moment, molecule by molecule.

As I wrote before, we returned to our camp around 2:00 P.M.; we immediately received orders to depart for the new position that our general had determined. Happily, we arrived without many surprises from the Italian air force and artillery.

---

31 A dogwood variety.

"We ... discovered the greenest valley full of blooming cornel-bushes and a loudly rolling creek ... We rested and enjoyed nature for a bit ..."

Our position now is 1035. It is a much safer position, although they continue to shell us. Fortunately they cannot see where the shells fall, so they can't correct their guns in order to hit us successfully. They also can't photograph us as they did before. We are so well camouflaged, there is no chance they'll see us; besides that, we have the fabulous green natural setting that was missing from our previous spot.

Yesterday I stayed in the general's tent, sharing quarters with his aide-de-camp Christodulos (who has the personality traits of Baron Munchausen); but today we set up our old tent with the wireless, and all is as before. Only instead of Officer Christodulos we have Mr. Gakis. Christodulos and the other captains have set up camp at the observation post. Today our general went there very early in the morning. He also asked for his bed and covers to be sent there because it is a forty-five-minute walk from our camp.

Just now we finished setting up our camp. I lit some candles and started logging the latest events.

I forgot to write that this morning the Italians began counter-

A downed Italian warplane. Dr. Electris is seated third from right.

attacking across the whole front. The fighting and the artillery duels are frighteningly hair-raising. They shake the earth, the whole planet, and up to this moment they are still firing.

It is now 7:15 P.M., and as our wireless operator is receiving the news, our guns (75 mm and 100 mm) are firing. The earth is trembling and so is the flame of the candle I've set on my bed. With every burst the brazier spits out its ashes on the ground ...

Now the firing has stopped and there is silence on both sides. Perhaps I'll sleep well tonight. I want to write to my wife, to whom I sent only a couple of cards the last two days; however, I have no news from her. I cannot forget the sweet moments I recalled from the fragrant piece of her stationary.

I forgot to write that during the air fight we saw a flaming airplane fall and two people in parachutes jump out.

Yesterday I smoked three cigarettes!

March 12, 1941

To be sick and to have to say that you are well ... I've been sick for two days now. The day before yesterday I had nightmares and a temperature higher than 40° C. Today I still am not well (37.6° C). On top of that I haven't eaten anything. I don't know how I got sick. Perhaps because I was digging when we were setting up our tents. Perhaps it's just the flu. I wrote to Chrysoula; I got her card in which she mentions things she has sent me that I have not received; they have been delayed somewhere.

Even with the fever, I'm going to try to eat some bean soup. What can I do, since I'm so weak?

March 15, 1941

My fever persists—last night it was 38.5. I'm completely exhausted and I don't know what to do. If I ask to go to the village they might misunderstand me; so I remain here. Fortunately my nurse brought for me from the village half a *kouramana* and 100 g of milk, which I'm going to drink now. It is about 11:30 A.M.

ITALIAN "PRIMAVERA" (SPRING) ATTACK
(9 MARCH 1941–15 MARCH 1941)

0   1   2   3   km

~~~~~ Line occupied by Greek forces

~~~~~ Line occupied by Italian forces

⟶ Italian directions of attack

- - - Line occupied by the Italians
      after the attack

Istore

Therepeli

ALPINE CHASSEURS   22

BLACK SHIRT

Bozout

Spathara

Lavdari

931

Mali Spadarit
1110

850

Boşketto

819

Dodovetsi

KAGLIARI   59   717

869

Bregou   Loulei

960

961

Boubessi   Saddle

Kiafe   Mourit

802

Kiafe   XI

Sialessi

800

1231

Nitsista

757

Hani Boubessi

Kiafe Sofiout

678

Boubessi

710

Bregou   Memoulazit

Toskitsi

1242

Golemi   38

XV   I

Mali Korap

PUGLIE

Monastero   717   Bregou

Rapit

XV   I

XV   I

Golemi

705

BLACK
SHIRT

731

Dras - e - Kai

Kaitsa   1123

Mali Tabayian

Fonde

Hani
Vinokazit

Tsouka   Fessik

Arza di Sotto

-1030

Balaban

24

-1060

I

PINEROLO

Hani
Balaban

Pavari

Maziani

Ronten

Selg

679

736

Arza di Mezzo

I   1306

630

I

Maritsai

XX   V   Psari

1425

Arza di Sopra

Mpali

Prol Tsepova R.

Trebessina

Tserogouni

Desnitsa R.

Souka

710

V

1816

Podgorani

Afhenas Metzgoranis

Goritsa

Apsos R.

See color version of this map on page 228.

I received Antonis' card, in which he repeatedly asks me to give him this diary when we see each other. He does not know that I plan to dedicate it to my little wife. Well, perhaps he'll have a part of it as well, though he won't be too satisfied because I don't know how to use the pen well ...

I'm not a writer, though as a physician and scientist, record keeping is part of my profession. However, writing this diary as well as all the card and letters really helps me psychologically; somehow it releases internal tensions, and pacifies me. Perhaps it helps me make sense out of this senseless catastrophic war, out of absurd and merciless death, out of doom and chaos. It helps me look for some bright light at the edge of darkness.

Sometimes at the brink of desperation I wonder why I do it, conscientiously and diligently write it. It is of no great literary value, and if we lose this war and our poor country ends up a battlefield again, it probably would be forgotten, even by me. If I'm killed and if the diary ever finds my wife, it might be a source of tears for her for the pain I endured and for our unrealized dreams ... Perhaps she will bury it in a chest and it will never see the light of day; but then again, she will know that a man loved her so much, that she was his idol and his goddess, his only source of light in the darkness. And perhaps, when she is very old, she will remember me again, and drag this yellowed document out to read it like a war adventure to her grandsons, even if they would not be mine.

Antonis also writes to me about courage and the importance of having faith in Victory. Faith in victory we all have, but courage is another story. Courage is very elusive, it escapes us and sometimes it takes a long time to come back to us. It especially vanishes when the shells and heavy missiles whistle over your head and the bombs from the planes explode next to you.

At this moment a heavy bomb of the 155-type (so big that two men could carry it only with great difficulty) whistled over my head and exploded on the opposite mountainside. Just now, as I'm scribing this comma, two more are exploding, one across from me and one to our side.

Each explosion on the mountain is such that you could compare it to the strongest wave ever heard breaking on the highest rocks during the greatest tempest ... but likening it to a storm diminishes its menace and somehow transforms it into some more familiar, less horrific experience of which we know, an experience that will pass.

Yesterday when we were being bombed by the airplanes, we were almost hit. How close to life is death!

All that I am and have done can be gone—poof—in an instant. Who will remember me then—my poor mother? The few patients I saved from death? My Chrysoula? Will I stay lodged in her mind's eye, encapsulated like an insect in a piece of amber? Have my illness and the bombing completely eroded my optimism?

Today the Italians attacked the advanced infantry trenches of the 8th and 13th companies. They advanced a great deal without being seen, but fortunately they were caught and repulsed.

Yesterday bombers destroyed the gun of the 14th Company and

Expecting a chemical attack.

wounded the telephone operator, a soldier and a sergeant. Another time the whole Economopoulos unit was endangered. The Italians also took Klissoura and advanced towards Nishitse, but fortunately they were thwarted there by our infantry.

How, then, can one not lose courage? How can one not be afraid, and stay brave? Such words are for the people who are not in the line of fire, academic words, words of Sunday evening tea among intellectuals and journalists.

There is a rumor that the damn Italians might start using gas warfare, for which we have no defense. Then we will all die.

March 16, 1941

My hair stood on end when I learned from my colleague Sites that when we were bombed three days ago our old site 1037 was bombed as well. The 14th Infantry gun that was there was hit—as I wrote before—but the very spot where our tent used to stand was directly hit and pulverized!

These days our soldiers do nothing besides digging trenches of varying depths. Unfortunately these trenches protect our men only from shell fragments. When the bombs hit, the explosion creates a hole more than two meters deep and covering an area as big as a tent.

Today I have asked Sites to examine me, since the fever persists and I don't know what the consequences might be.

His diagnosis was that I had the flu.

Today I took a laxative. My temperature in the morning was 37.9°C and my pulse is not good. Nevertheless, I seem to be getting better. I shaved and the shadow of illness began to disappear. I feel very exhausted however, all over my body.

No mail today and I have had no chance to write to my wife. Now I will try to answer some of the letters and cards I have received. I will start with Nitsa and Elli first.

March 20, 1941

Yesterday my fever broke and was down to normal, but the exhaustion still remains. My recovery is slow because my appetite is gone. All food tastes awful and bitter.

Today Officer Xanthopoulos is going home because he has been wounded by a shell fragment. He is going to pass by my house and I will give him whatever is supposed to go to my wife. Some of it is my heavy winter clothes, so I'll have one less box to haul around. Whatever it is, though, my sweetheart is going to be so happy to receive something of mine. I'll write her a letter to tell her to expect it.

March 22, 1941

Many times funny things happen at the front and lots of anecdotes go around. One of the strange things is that, while the Greeks and the Italians hit each other wherever they meet, and no one dares to stick his nose out unprotected for fear of getting shot, there is one place where the following peculiar thing happens.

The top of this mountain is neutral because one side of it is occupied by the Italians and the other by the Greeks. No one dares go up on top; even the occasional helmet that might be thrown in the air, for jest, is invariably turned into a colander by bullets. However, the mountain has no water other than a spring in an adjoining ravine. Strangely enough, both Greeks and Italians descend to that spring with their canteens, unarmed, and take turns filling them up—after greeting each other politely!

Other stories go around about the extra nerve that the Greek soldier finds in order to come up with food and loot.

In one occasion a soldier had nothing to eat—as is common—except for one dried piece of *kouramana*. It was Mardi Gras time and he was not going to pass it with a dried piece of bread. Nearby there was an unoccupied village that was being shelled by both sides. In the village, though, there were supplies and especially sacks of maize that occasional daring souls would dare to loot and roast on their mess-tin covers. Our soldier now decided that he was going to supply himself with some of that corn. He told his friends that he was going to the village to have Mardi Gras. He came to this house and opened the door, only to discover three Italians seated around a table, eating. His hunger overcame his better instincts; his gut grumbled, and his determination to fill it made him a giant in front of the three Italian soldiers, who immediately got up from the table saying "Bono Greco." He, gaining more courage, sat at the table and started eating their food, and also had the audacity to send one of the soldiers to bring him some water! No one knows how they communicated, but after filling himself he shared the rest with the three Italians who, after eating, followed him to the Greek lines. His friends, who had seen him leaving alone, saw him return with three prisoners of war!

The Greek soldier is the consummate war looter. His courage triples when it comes to prime looting. A few days ago the Italians attacked one of the trenches of the 13th and 6th units. It was a surprise attack, and many of our soldiers started running. One of those who was running, in the midst of incredible shelling, realized that the fallen Italian behind him was an officer. Well, the rascal had the guts to return, amidst all the shelling and with great composure amidst the crossfire, to sit and fleece, from hair to toenail, the fallen Italian officer. After taking the man's wallet and gun and pen and knife and boots, he had the audacity, with great coolness, to cut off his finger and remove his ring! This looting will drive these soldiers to such an extreme that rather than retreat they will endanger their lives for the sake of it.

March 24, 1941

Last night we had to decontaminate all of our personal belongings, including our uniforms. Though I had no lice this time, I had to undergo this trouble just to be on the safe side. It was an annoying experience because I had to wait for about an hour and a half for all my belongings to be decontaminated, in two batches. For hours the soldiers hung around the decontamination chambers, some naked, some half naked, some wrapped up in blankets. I would have taken some pictures, but it was getting too dark.

I had Syropoulos take all my undergarments to the village to be washed. The milk that was brought to me from town was spoiled, but my wife's candy is giving me extra nourishment. Today I have to look for some extra food because I could not eat the bean soup when I found a worm in it.

In the afternoon I visited the 4th Artillery and had some pictures taken with the other officers and doctors. I smoked a few cigarettes—three. I'm beginning to get used to them and it does not seem strange to me that I'm smoking.

Tomorrow is the 25th of March, our Independence Day. Who knows what is waiting out there for us ...

March 27, 1941
My beloved Phaedia,

Not even today did I receive a card! The last news was from the 19th, from the soldier who stopped by the house. I learned about the air battles over your positions and I'm doubly worried. With each card I send I say:

Quickly to go
Quickly to come
To bring back
The man I love

But it is all in vain. I can see your smile under your mustache thinking how silly I am. Now, another unbearable thing I have to do is leave, with the rest of the family, for an island. I have to go with them because they won't go without me. I do not want to endanger everyone.

Before I started packing and putting away our valuable things, I took care of all your medical tools by rubbing them with alcohol and coating them with Vaseline. I was instructed to do this by one of your nurses.

March 29, 1941

It is the first day of the sixth month since the day we were mobilized, and the day we parted. It is horrible to think that so many months have gone by; the memories of our parting are still so fresh.

I got a letter from home from my mother. She describes to me how happy they were to see my pictures ... I got some peace of mind that my sister Sofia is being taken care of and that my father has sent everyone to Katerini, though he still remains in Thessaloniki. I hope, though, that they will all get together and that my brother George will not be drafted.

Here all is stagnant. We haven't seen any bombers for at least a week, and today only two small bombers passed over us. We are expecting with great anxiety the fall of Tepeleni; and since the morale of the Italians is so low and the Serbs are fighting the Germans, we can easily defeat them with a general assault.

Meanwhile the 11th Unit has been replaced by the 6th from Serres. Our artillery, though, still remains. There was a rumor that the 3rd Squadron was going to be replaced and we hoped that we also would be replaced, but perhaps we would have been sent to some unknown situation. The war is everywhere and the unknown perhaps is worse than what surrounds us here and now, even if it is shelling from the Italian heavy artillery.

Just now I received a letter from my uncle in Katahas—he has invited my family to go stay with him.

March 30, 1940

This morning I'm answering my wife's letters from the 22nd and 24th sitting in the dugout shelter. The Italians have gone crazy with their heavy artillery. They are trying to break our nerve. Now their bombers are going crazy as well.

My sweet wife's letter is full of sadness and worry because they have to leave Thessaloniki.

Meanwhile, for the last four days I have been suffering from severe migraine and a sinus infection. I have no appetite but I force myself to eat, little by little, so that I will regain my previous strength.

April 3, 1941

April brought us an irregularity in the mail service. Our division has left Nishitse and has been replaced by the 6th Division from Serres. Of its squadrons only the 11th Element, the staff and our squadron remain in their old posts. We now have the 6th Division's mail code: 415. Fortunately, I have warned my wife about the irregularities in the mail.

On the first of April I took a short walk to the observation post. The weather changed suddenly as I walked, and I was caught in a pelting, driving rain. Today, though, I gathered wild daisies from the opposite mountainside and asked the soldiers to bring me a branch from a white blooming tree. From far away the tree looked like an almond tree, but it was a wild crabapple tree with the fragrance of honey.

I put the crabapple branch together with a blooming cornel branch in a bottle, and now, on top of my medical supplies box there are two vases of white daisies and violets and, in the middle, the bottle of crabapple and cornel flowers—instant happiness!

I do not know how this expedition is going to end. Things are getting more complicated with the German threat. Fortunately Serbia is on our side. We haven't seen Italian bombers for a while. This is a very happy thing, but it really does not matter much because all I want is my wife, my home ... I long so much for everyone ...

I wonder if the family ever left for Katahas.

April 6, 1941

New war, new allies and new adventure, and a good start for all with 500 German prisoners. We'll have to wait and see if we are going to be lucky in the end.

Today, after six days without mail, I received a letter from my wife and a letter from my sister Sofia. My wife writes that they might go to Evia. I'm anxious to learn where they will end up.

The last few days we were very desperate with no new mail or newspapers. I kept myself busy reading the medical guide we received a few days ago on chemical and gas warfare. It will be a com-

Trenches overlook the opposing heights.

plete disaster if the Italians or the Germans use them; we have no defense against them.

So far it is very quiet along the front. Perhaps the Italians are focusing their efforts along the Serbian border. We cannot advance any further because we are already very far advanced. We are waiting for Tepeleni, or better, for the mountains around Tepeleni to fall. No one is occupying the town of Tepeleni. I hope that the big fighting is going to commence soon now that Serbia is in the war. Perhaps the Greek army will try to surround the Italians by going through Serbia, or the Serbs will chase them all the way to the sea. If so, in about one month we will rid Albania of the Italians.

April 8, 1941

Yesterday the spring rains started again. It rained all night and until 10:00 this morning. It was damp and cold, so I had to put on my warm winter socks and two sweaters over the blue sleeveless one that my wife had made. Certainly, though, it's just a passing rain.

The observation post.

After the rain the delicate lace of the young spring leaves glitters in the sun. The warmth of the sun brings a green explosion. We need the leaf coverage for protection from both the enemy and the sun. The leaves are the best camouflage for protecting us from the "milkman's" visits.

Yesterday the Serbs attacked the Italians in Skorda and the poor guys don't know what retreat road to take. They can't even escape by sea, since the English and Greek Navies are waiting for them.

Today we are expecting the mail. I'm anxiously awaiting a letter from my wife to learn if she received the money and the packages I sent her. Yesterday Mr. Sambingikos left and I sent a film with him to give to my family. I think that he will at least find my father.

April 9, 1941

Two hours ago I received huge and horrible news, first from a German radio station and then from a British one:

Thessaloniki has been occupied!

I feel cold sweat all over my body. I don't know if my wife has left Thessaloniki or not. I'm not so worried that she would have been hurt by the Germans had she stayed in Thessaloniki; after all, the Germans are considered to be disciplined soldiers. I'm more concerned that she will die of agony because she will not be able to communicate with me.

Around 8:30 the mailman brings me two of her letters, numbers 34 and 35. They are still in Thessaloniki as of the 29th, and she does not know if they can leave. I'm worried, now I don't know where they will be.

That "worry" again; it is a parasitic organism, an evil goddess that claws our guts and the inside of our skulls, killing us little by little.

I read the letter and the words take on their own meaning, other than what she intended them to have.

At one point she writes: " ... today for sure you will get some good news."

Indeed we got news, but it is not good:

THESSALONIKI HAS FALLEN!

April 10, 1941
My sweetest little wife,

What can I do, I must answer your letters of March 6, 7, 8 & 9. I am very sad, but I do not know where you are. In your letter of the 31st you tell me that things are getting better in Thessaloniki and you are not sure whether you will leave. Now—eight days later—I read your letter and Thessaloniki has fallen. I'm afraid that you haven't been able to leave and so we will lose every contact, even the precious one of correspondence.

My Chrysoula, my sweetest wife, my heart gets tight with this thought, and it stops with the thought that you will be suffering without my news. Oh, if only, just by thought, I could transfer these words to you: I'm O.K. Today I will write to my mother and Evridiki and tell them of my pain and ask them to write to me about your whereabouts.

My darling, I don't doubt at all the things you write to me in your letter and I want to believe that I was able to make you happy. My sweet Chrysoula, how sad I am that I was not able to make your happiness complete. Our life together stopped so abruptly, so unexpectedly, before we had even begun it.

Don't worry, I won't discuss with either you or your father my concerns that you are being faced with unexpected responsibilities. I recognize in you a strong, whole, independent individual extremely capable of facing any difficult situation.

My darling, the mustache and cigarettes I will have only when I'm far away from you. I try to forget myself as I twist my mustache and try to make rings with the golden smoke. When I will be with you again, my love, will be greater than before.

I thank you for your last package with my glasses and the toothpaste, pen and chocolates. I'm sorry that you haven't received the money and things I sent you with my fellow officer.

Anyway, my Chrysoula, my thoughts are concentrated on you! Now it is half past midnight, I listened to the news and will try to write a letter to my sister and then try to sleep.

Good night, my love, and sweet dreams and countless kisses to you ...
Your darling husband Phaedia
P.S. Greetings to Mother, Andromahi, Popi, Nitsa, Elli and Father.

April 11, 1941

It has been snowing since this morning and it won't stop—big, fat snowflakes. It was so cold that I did not want to get up from under my covers. Around 11:00 A.M., though, I heard the treasurer. He paid me for April. I know that I cannot send the money to my wife, but I can at least send it to my mother and my sister Sofia.

April 13, 1941

Yesterday at 8:15 many Italians gathered and shouted, "Hurrah for the Greeks, long live the Greeks" and other similar things. That is only because the day before they tried a counterattack that failed. It seemed that they had decided to try some other sneaky tactics such as they are accustomed to. In return they received some fruits of the 75 mm guns from the 4th Artillery.

The news from Thessaloniki is somewhat reassuring regarding our families. The German general, to whom the keys to the city have been surrendered, declared that he guaranteed complete safety and peace for all the residents of the city. Just as I expected, the Germans are not like the Italians and the Bulgarians.

The most unbelievable thing, though, like an April Fools' joke, is that the snow that started to fall has continued for three days. Everything is covered, and the trees look as if they have been wrapped in cotton. I hope I can get some pictures.

Finally last night it stopped. There was a full moon and the stars sparkled. Around 10:00 P.M. I had to visit a patient in the 3rd Artillery, Sergeant Zographos. Despite the mud I enjoyed the walk. It was magic as the moon transformed the trees into spun gold and the air was fresh and crisp, a lift of the soul.

So the next day's sun and thaw were almost certain. I succeeded in sending a letter to my sister and my brother-in-law Nikos, who was at the front. I'm anxiously awaiting a letter from Chrysoula. I hope that she has not left Thessaloniki; I will be sad if our nest is spoiled.

I have a feeling that I will see her soon.

April 14, 1941

Yesterday, the Italian Easter, they would not give us any peace. They continue to try our nerves by attacking us. Our squadron was obliged to fire back. The other units are short of ammunition, so they do not fire. There are rumors that our squadron will be moved, so they fire in order to lighten up the ammunition. Besides the annoyance from the Italian attacks, we are worried about our city, which has been isolated by the Germans. We have no contact with our homes. I can't hide it: at best I'm pessimistic about the whole situation. I don't know what the others are thinking; I suspect they are thinking the same as I do, but they do not want to show it, and at the last minute they will panic.

I'm thinking of the worst possible situation. So I have cleared out my correspondence, kept only my little wife's letters and a few from my parents, which can, if worse comes to worst, be put in a pocket. I will try to send money to my mother to secure at least something for them.

As for my things, I'll carry what I can on my back, and the medical supplies and blankets on Sideris' back.

Just now a new commander has arrived, Major Fyntikakis. He is replacing Lieutenant-Colonel Drungas. I have been hearing the rumors of the replacement go around for days now, but he himself never told me. I know that he was sorry to leave us, since we went through so many things together.

Last night I read the official notice from the XI Division that I am to receive a medal for exceptional deeds. About a month ago I got an honorable mention from the division.

The new commander has impressed me and his presence gives me courage.

Chrysoula is in my mind. I have no news from Thessaloniki. I don't know where she is.

April 14, 1941 (6:00 P.M.)

About an hour ago we were ordered to pack our things and get ready to depart at about 9:00 P.M. So much effort, hardship and trial, so many glories, so much blood, and now we are marching towards the unknown, ignorant of what is waiting for us and what the outcome of our new tribulations will be. Everyone is sad and grieving. We are victorious, we fought for every rock and piece of earth beneath our feet, we soaked it with our blood, we left our young unburied there to rot, we hoped that our future would be laurels and songs of glory and church bells and decorations, but now what? What is out there for us is utterly unknown!

Now I have all surrounding me, Karamoshos and Sideris and all the rest. No words can come out of my mouth, but they all know what I want to say.

I wish my love will protect me and guide me to get close to her.

Dr. Electris with Lieutenant-Colonel Drungas.

Members of the XI artillery group and one of their guns.

The flowers I put in the bottle on the first day of the German attack are still blooming.

I'm sad I'm leaving them as well ...

April 15, 1941 (Good Tuesday)

Last night, at exactly 8:30 P.M., we started from the Spandara [Nichice] complex or camp with orders to move towards Rehovista, Prishte, Cepane and Roka. I cannot describe this torturous journey. We walked nonstop for at least 12 hours, till dawn or later. Finally we arrived at a position where many infantry divisions from Serres, and other cavalry and mountaineering divisions, were gathered. There was incredible noise and hubbub. We camped on the left side of the site. I tried to push all oppressive thoughts away from my mind and I looked for something pleasant, some good omen.

There were some trees that were blooming; some were white and some had small purple-pink flowers like those of beans. The trees reminded me of the acacia trees outside the post office in Harilaou.[32] A thought of home—a good omen?

---

32 A suburb of Thessaloniki.

I spread my blankets and tent underneath the tree. I looked up at it trying to focus on positive thoughts. The tree had not leafed yet. Lying there for three hours I tried desperately to go to sleep. Though I was exhausted, I could not. My legs and feet were killing me.

Meanwhile, I saw Evnouhides coming towards me, looking exhausted. He was looking for his hostler and his things. He pleaded with me to let him rest next to me on my blankets. We both lay down for a long time, but no sleep came.

I thought that if I washed my feet they would feel better and I could go to sleep. My feet felt better all right, but still no sleep.

We ate some halvah and bread hoping that would help. Before we left we packed supplies for three days. Along the way I tried nourishing myself by eating the almonds and biscuits that my wife and mother had sent. Now I got up so Sideris could tie up the blankets. I'm lying on top of the tent hoping to finally get some sleep. It is about 5:00 A.M.; we have to wait and see what the day will have in store for us.

April 16, 1941

We started off again around 7:00 P.M., leaving Roka. Fortunately, it was still light enough so that we could see where we were going. Our climb was incredible, and it would have been almost impossible to do had it been dark. I was totally exhausted from the march and the lack of sleep and food. I had a very hard time eating. As we climbed, I was running out of breath and getting very sweaty. I tried to make a lot of stops and drink plenty of water. Perhaps I was out of shape from sitting around for two months at the camps.

I forgot to write that after 9:00 P.M. our phalanx marched with lit torches. So a person standing at the bottom by the river could see, all the way to the top of the mountain along the ravine, a lit procession. Ironically, we are accustomed to such torch-lit processions on Easter days. It is literally Passion Week for us as well.

Last year this time I started to participate in family gatherings as a new member of my wife's family. I remember that I followed

Chrysoula together with the others into the church, not because I was taken over by the great religious spirit but just to please my little love. I knew that it was great satisfaction for her, especially because whispers of our engagement were going around. And I would follow my love anywhere because she was now my devotion, my religion ...

Well, I'm digressing from the problem at hand.

At around 11:00 P.M. one of the guns overturned and fell down the ravine, so we all stopped. The place where my hostler, my nurses and I stopped was on a steep incline, but we successfully unloaded our equipment and tried to camp there for the night. One of my nurses, Karamoshos, was pitiful. He had great difficulty walking, had heart palpitations, and he was on the verge of collapse. I carried his load for 20 minutes and tried to load it on a horse. I walked with him, talking to him, trying to encourage him as much as I could.

I had to get some sleep, so I chose a spot about 500 m away from the rest of the men and asked my hostler to lay down blan-

One of the bridges that Dr. Electris crossed.

kets for me. Well, wouldn't you know it, it started raining. I quickly covered myself with my raincoat and slept atop the wet blankets. Evnouhides found me and was nudging up to me trying to share my covers, but I pretended that I did not know that he was there and did not budge. I had to get some sleep this time. What could I do? In war one cannot give away his ammunition.

April 17, 1941

I slept wonderfully despite the rain and the wet covers, and so I recovered my strength to continue the march. In the morning we started around 7:00 A.M. for the longest march to date. We walked continuously for over 20 hours, walked 50 km and did not stop until 3:30 the next morning.

From that time on, things happened continuously and fast, faster than the rushing rivers that we crossed. The seconds ran into minutes and the minutes melted into hours; the days and nights fused into a continuum, time careening forward so rapidly that we could not hear our hearts beat, carrying us along in a sort of free fall to an unknown, unexpected confusing course of events. Immediate actions and quick decisions were required at every moment, on every front; standards of decent behavior seemed to vanish and people seemed to be looking out only for themselves instead of the whole.

But let me begin at the beginning:

First we passed all the villages (four exactly) of the so-called Sevranochoria (the villages of Sevran). As we dragged ourselves through the mud and rain, we felt as though we were experiencing Christ's passion. This walk made it impossible for me to put anything in my mouth. Happily, in the last village I'd had two thin slices of bread with a little piece of cheese and emptied two whole canteens of water that our sergeant major had given me.

I will never forget what happened as we marched from the last village towards Tapani.

We met up with a company of infantrymen who had just cooked some warm rice with cod, and they were handing it out to the passing soldiers, perhaps because they had some extra. Certainly the combination of rice and cod sounded bizarre, but just the idea of warm food suddenly appealed to me and I could not pass up the opportunity. So, I sent Sideris to get some and he filled a mess tin. We all fell on it and started eating it like animals. I could not believe I was eating this rice, I who could not stand to even look at it lately. My survival instincts took hold of me! We walked and ate at the same time because we could not stop. As we passed by, the Albanians standing at their doors looked at us with great curiosity and amazement. Perhaps they were saying, "How hungry these poor officers are!" My manner of eating was adopted by many others because no one could stop.

The phalanx moved in a serpentine way, and along its sides equipment was scattered everywhere. Ammunition and supplies were pushed into the ravines, because it was impossible to move it all. The decomposing carcasses of dead horses and mules were scattered everywhere; the stench at some places was unbearable.

Meanwhile the march went forward. We started to encounter better paths where the ground was solid and in places covered with grass. Then all was green and on the right and left of us there were arbutus bushes blooming in the sun, oblivious to the snaking phalanx that unfolded noisily with a hubbub alongside them. For a flash of a second, as the corner of my eye caught them, I was envious of them. They had no worries, no expectations, no disappointments, no loves waiting for them.

We finally descended towards a valley and we found ourselves in a small grove of blooming bushes and other plants with white flowers, and a small flat area full of green grass next to a loudly roaring river. Here the whole division had a stop. Wow! What a sight! What a gift to our tired souls, a miracle to behold! We had descended from hell to paradise ... (unfortunately I had no camera to make this sight eternal.)

All along the march I became quite friendly with our commander—especially today after I told him a few off-color jokes. In a while, after the men and animals had rested, we started again towards the bridge of the public road. We crossed the river twice and went through a green valley covered with flowers. All along the way the road was littered with blankets, backpacks and other equipment. Finally we crossed the bridge about 11:10 P.M. and took the road towards Premeti. We walked and walked and walked and finally, around 3:30 A.M., we arrived at our destination.

April 18, 1941

We arranged our things as best we could in the dark and lay down trying to get some shut-eye for a few hours. I put up the stretcher and my supply boxes all around and made an extensive sleeping arrangement with blankets on the bottom and my raincoat as a top cover. I slept well and deeply because I was so extremely tired.

This morning we were supposed to stay in Premeti, a big village with nice houses, but my group and I decided to stay two kilometers outside the village and began to set up our tents. We had some tea and I shared the little sugar I had with the boys. We learned that there were good supplies of food, so I sent my hostler to get some provisions. We saw the Albanians running around carrying anything one's heart could desire, from whole slaughtered lambs, which they were carrying on their shoulders, to halvah and pasta and gasoline. They were carrying all these things to safe places. They were going to have a plentiful Easter.

In any case, my hostler came back with a bunch of kidneys that I fried in animal fat. Of course I had the first bite, then our commander, then Christopoulos, then the rest.

My tent was all set up, and our supplies were all gathered and we were ready to lie down when an order came that we were supposed to start moving again at 6:00 P.M.

At 5:00 P.M. Karamoshos came and took one of our four animals. I had to rearrange all the loads again. I told our commander that it was extremely difficult to try to carry all of the supplies and that we had to abandon some. The commander told me to do whatever I thought was right. So, unfortunately, I emptied two of the boxes and used alcohol and ether to light them up. The explosions of the bottles and the sound drew a big crowd around the site.

I told all the amazed soldiers that, all along, their doctor had the ammunition and could destroy things at will.

As we were loading it started raining. We were given raisins and olives for food supplies along the way and finally we started off around 7:00 P.M.

We walked on a paved road. The mountains shot up on either side of the road, immense and snow-covered, and down the road we could see the river Aoos.

We stopped at the first bridge because on the other side of it, on the road that stretched along the base of the mountain, marched an endless column of soldiers. We took our turn and joined the column.

There was still light, and we had a chance to admire the majestic wilderness of that sight. On the other side of the river, up high and through the clouds, the white houses of a village sparkled among majestic black cypress trees.

Ah, well, beautiful villages, rivers, bridges, roads—they all had cost our people money and were soaked in their blood, and all this for nothing—all these roads and bridges will be blown up by our engineering divisions.

We walked until we got to the bridge at Petrani. It wasn't a very long march; after settling all our things (and that takes a long time), it was only 11:30 P.M.

I forgot to write that Sergeant Zographos told me that at the first bridge we stopped at yesterday, my brother-in-law, Nikos, was looking for me. We had never met before, since he was away in the army when I got married. When we stopped at the bridge, I was in the beginning of our column, and I had my helmet on; besides, I have grown a mustache and a beard. I was very sorry to have missed him there, but somehow I had a premonition that I was still going to see him.

Indeed, later in the day I heard my name being called from a passing military vehicle. It was Nikos! We kissed each other and talked for a while. I gave him 12,000 dr. that I had on me, because his group was going to be the first to arrive on Greek soil. They were going to Ioannina and I asked him to send the money to my wife or to my sister Evridiki. We kissed again, but in the excitement I forgot to take a picture of the two of us. Now he is gone; I wish him well with all my heart.

We started out again at 9:00 in the morning, walked for 7 km and then stopped among some trees. The artillery had to line up to cover and defend all the retreating troops. It is rumored that we will have a long walk today and we will eventually find ourselves on Greek ground. This morning we took a picture as soon as we woke up and then again with Dr. Papathanasiou. We were drafted together at the beginning of the war.

I also forgot to write that our commander made a huge mistake. He sent 30 animals and a group of men 20 km to an area near Perati [Perat], 2 km sw of Merjani, for supplies. He made the whole artillery unit wait 5 hours on Albanian soil while the command division moved ahead. It was a mistake because we had plenty of food and, besides, no one was interested in eating after all that marching. Also, we knew that we could get other supplies 15 km from the spot we were in. I just don't get the point of that move. Perhaps he wanted to show that he cared for our artillery and wanted them to be well supplied.

In any case, it meant extra hard and fast marching for us, because we had to catch up with the command unit.

We left around 8:00 p.m., and, as we were moving from the Albanian soil, we felt more and more relieved.

On the road there were endless convoys. The paved road was about 5 m wide and on the left and right side of the road the soldiers were marching on foot, while the animals were in the middle line. One could hear every kind of joke and people calling for friends and comrades. Calls like, "Is anyone from Tepeleni here?" or, "Anyone from Tria Avga?" or, "Guys—anyone from Verati?"

It is strange, but everyone seemed to be marching as though they thought that they were going back to their towns. In fact, I'm sure that if they'd been told to fight instead of going home, they would have refused. They had no desire to fight for some capitalistic cause that was not in the interest of the people. Widespread confusion prevailed about what was really happening. We did really defeat the

Italians, but what was really happening now? Why were our spirits so broken? Why did some of us look back with nostalgia at those cruel mountainsides and ravines? Were we looking for justice from the gods, for those fair gods to crown us with laurels? Anyway, who said that the gods were fair, or that they cared or had anything to do with us pitiful mortals?

An incident that happened among the soldiers of the 31st Regiment is indicative of the fact that people did not want to fight anymore.

When an officer of the 31st ordered the soldiers of the company to march toward the enemy to fight, he got a refusal. The soldiers refused to move and said that they did not want to get killed but only wanted to go back home. Then the same officer ordered another company to fire against his group. Two soldiers were killed in the subsequent skirmish.

Fortunately the general got involved and things calmed down. One could hear the shouts of the soldiers of that regiment calling, "Long live the general!"

The whole 67th Regiment was overjoyed when the general addressed the soldiers and told them that they were all going to go to their homes, but then he added: "But first we will repulse the attackers and fight the enemy to the end!"

That was the last straw and many of the soldiers started hollering: "We won't fight," and "We don't fight!"

The general asked the captain to find out who exactly were the people that shouted, "We don't fight!"

Other captains held private discussions with their soldiers to try to find out who had been doing the shouting. What they found instead was that no soldier wanted to fight.

The soldiers' spirits and psychological states were reported to the upper command divisions; the commander was replaced by one who was friendly with the soldiers and who appeased them by telling them that no soldier's life was going to be at risk.

I have to return now to our march. As I wrote before, it was a hasty and rushed one. In charge of us was Second Lieutenant Nikolaides. As we marched, some other division came along the left side

Dr. Electris at the river Aoos. "There was still light, and we had a chance to admire the majestic wilderness of that sight."

"This morning we took a picture as soon as we woke up and then again with Dr. Papathanasiou. We were drafted together at the beginning of the war."

of the road and tried to push us aside. When we came to the bridge at Mesogephira, they tried to stop us, take our turn, and cross the bridge. Nikolaides almost gave in to the demands of the commander of the other division. Seeing that all our horses were in danger of falling off the road as we were being pushed aside, I could not stand in silence. I started arguing with the commander of the other division, who was encouraging his soldiers to push us off and go across the bridge. Finally, after seeing that we had no intention of giving up our turn, he retreated and waited for us to cross.

We crossed the bridge and stepped onto GREEK SOIL at 3:20 A.M.

A different kind of air was blowing and a different kind of courage came over us! We all stopped and breathed deeply the Hellenic air. It was a bittersweet celebration, however. Some of these rough fighters knelt down and kissed the mother ground, others took some soil in their hands and rubbed it on their faces or put it in their helmets. Some people were crying as they walked; others cried sitting down. Some were looking back at the Albanian lands and others were showing their fists as they were looking back. Some were singing and rejoicing, finding new strength for a coming march even longer than the one we had just completed!

An hour later we stopped and camped again. I went with the command unit to the river shore, where there were some trees, and lay on top of my covers as before.

April 19, 1941

I slept without knowing for how long. When I woke up, the sun had been out for awhile. I made some tea and had a little something to eat. Zographos and I had been talking for a while when the German bombers appeared and started shelling and bombing us. These guys are really good; unlike the Italians, they are not afraid of the anti-aircraft guns.

It appears that we are going to remain here, waiting for the rest of the artillery unit that was sent to get the supplies.

April 20, 1941

Today we spent the whole day resting. For lunch they cooked beans for us and gave each of us two oranges. For dinner we are going to have meat.

The plan is for us to move again around 9:00 P.M.

Unfortunately we've had many visits—from German planes. Everywhere you look, there are planes coming from all directions. It appears that they are trying to break our morale. Some of the planes dropped sacks of food; others, paper declarations for the Greek soldiers. Some got down very low, as low as 50 m; we could see the pilots. If they wanted to they could have shelled us, because they could see us very well. I'm beginning to hate these guys.

During our retreat we had to let all the Italian prisoners of war go free so that we would not have to haul them along. These prisoners were taken during the last Italian assault against the Greeks, which had failed. We had captured many and, after disarming them, we were holding them. Now they are all free.

April 21, 1941

Yesterday we were supposed to leave at 9:00 P.M. But we were ordered to stay here and defend the retreat of the 6th Division, although it was not our turn but that of the Voudouklari Squadron. I spent an agonizing night. There was a lot of whispering about deserting, and many actually took off in groups. Syropoulos got away from me and so did Pontikas, together with someone else. Up to about three o'clock in the morning I could hear people running on the road. The same spirit prevailed everywhere. Nobody wanted to fight.

I met up with Zographos, who was going to the command quarters. It was 3:00 A.M. and he told me that our government has changed and that we have asked for a truce!

Very early in the morning I was shaken out of my half-asleep state by loud voices and great cheers. I ran out to the road and learned that indeed a truce had been signed! People were shooting in the air, and some colonel from the infantry spoke and told the soldiers about the truce; he told the soldiers to clean up and make themselves decent so that the Germans would not find them in such sad shape.

I was elated, though I could not really believe it! Even now I can't find words to write what I felt. It was a moment I had waited for since the first day of this expedition, but why was I simultaneously experiencing this deadly sadness, this overwhelming heavy feeling, as if someone had died?

Perhaps it was a feeling that we have lost the war, though we knew fully well that we had won all or most of the battles with the blood of our souls.

Perhaps it was a fear of what was going to happen next, or of the unknown ... I think I will carry these feelings with me forever, like a giant scar in the middle of my chest. Though I haven't been wounded, I have been scarred for life.

I shaved and cut my hair and anxiously waited for further developments. What joy would my Chrysoula experience! With what joy will everyone be expecting me, my mother, my brother and sisters.

Time: 10:30 P.M.
After lunch this afternoon I tried to get some sleep and awoke around 6:00 P.M. to some very unpleasant news. Karamoshos told me that the captain had ordered all available men to go to the artillery positions with their guns. The soldiers refused to join the artillery under any conditions. They were worried that they would end up with the infantry in the defense line.

The Italians started new hostilities as soon as they learned that Greece had signed a truce with Germany. It seems that they are attempting to occupy as much ground as they can. I and the other officers, who had no desire to go to the artillery position, tried to persuade our soldiers not to desert but at the same time not go to the artillery position, but stay put where they were and wait for further developments. Unfortunately no one was listening. Even Sideris and Syropoulos, who had returned from their first attempt to desert, were getting ready to leave again. I was very upset and it looked as if I was going to be left alone without my support group.

But then, just miraculously at 9:00 P.M., as everyone was beginning to leave, we saw a German motorized division moving down the road!

The would-be deserters all came to their senses and got very quiet!

The German occupation is now at our borders!

At 9:30 P.M. we got an order to prepare for departure as soon as the artillery joins us. In about ten days we will be back in our homes.

What a joy for our tired souls!

We will depart from here at 1:00 A.M.; it appears that we will surrender all our supplies and guns in Ioannina.

April 23, 1941

Yesterday morning we finally started off around 2:00 A.M. and arrived at the 49th km[33] without any complications at about 8:00 A.M. There are rumors that we are going to have to walk all the way to Thessaloniki, so I bought myself a mule that was not part of our unit. At the 49th km we met up with our division and together we marched (leaving at 1:00 A.M.) and got to the 34th km by 7:30 A.M. Now, after that last 15 km march, I'm lying exhausted on top of a military bed so I can rest, because we probably will start moving again around noon.

There are rumors and rumors and many of them worry me.

It is being said that they are going to take us to Preveza and load us onto boats headed towards an unknown destination. It is being whispered that some of the professional officers refused to sign the truce and want to fight and stop the Germans. What they don't know, though, is that among the common soldiers there is no one who will follow them to fight the Germans.

Ah, well, things will settle down when the last of our guns and weapons have been turned over to the Germans.

I'm anxious to get to Ioannina and send my news to Chrysoula.

---

33 Distances were marked on the roads.

April 25, 1941

The officers above us deceived us for one whole day. Their reasons were that we had to surrender our guns to the Germans at Ioannina. However, that was not a real reason but only a pretext.

The real reason was that they were trying to keep us longer. To what end? I don't really know. Maybe they were feeling sorry about losing the guns and wanted us to hold on to them. How could that be, when the whole land around Ioannina and for many kilometers beyond was a cemetery of scattered military equipment? We couldn't believe what we saw with our eyes as we passed through: guns, tents, swords, grenades, cannons, saddles ... Except for the healthy horses that the soldiers rode as they were leaving for their towns and villages, they abandoned everything.

I tried to send a card to Chrysoula telling her that they planned for us to march towards Thessaloniki. Those in command above us are trying to do something with the soldiers who remain. As to what that is, we have no idea. The soldiers have no intention of fighting, especially after seeing the warmonger Officer Baltas desert on the first day of our march towards Ioannina, as well as Christopoulos and Zographos and other officers and soldiers.

In the afternoon the commander of the division spoke to us. He said that we were considered prisoners of war and that we had to remain outside Ioannina. He said that the Italians were occupying Metsovo. The Germans, who wanted to sleep in peace, did not allow any movement, and if they caught anyone walking or moving about, they would arrest him and take him to a concentration camp. He also told us that if we tried to go towards Metsovo we would be in danger of being arrested by the Italians. However, the Italians were at the 8th km from Ioannina, in Kalpaki.

Towards evening those above us saw that the soldiers were shaken and unsettled and decided it was time to surrender the guns. They took all of us in a different direction, as far as possible, toward the village of Bafra[34] [Prosfyges].

There we found milk and yogurt and eggs. Meanwhile, the guns

---

34 A village southwest of Ioannina near the town of Neokesaria.

*A receipt from the mayor of Bafra for
medical supplies returned by Dr. Electris.*

were being moved farther and farther away.

Earlier we had decided not to turn in our medical equipment for fear we would be recognized as doctors and kept as hostages. I let Sideris leave with his brother. Then the other doctor and I agreed that it was time for us to leave, so I turned all medical supplies in to the village mayor and took off.

Karamoshos, Syropoulos (who had already left and come back twice) and I walked for 23 km outside Ioannina and camped out for the night. We were rained on as we were sleeping. All around us people were moving and running away. No one was staying.

April 26, 1941

We started off in the morning with four mules, and at the 46th km we found a very inhospitable village. We ate a few leeks with some butter and split an egg three ways. We will take different roads, some towards Kalambaka and some towards Preveza. Around 4:30 P.M. we found ourselves in Metsovo trying to secure some supplies for ourselves and the animals. Unfortunately there were so many armies, both Greek and German, that we got nothing except some hay for the mules for 50 dr.

We wanted to get out of there as soon as possible because rumor had it that the Germans were looking for Greek officers, especially because they wanted to take all their things for loot. (Later that rumor turned out to be true.)

I hid my wedding ring and some money I had, and we slithered out of the village square as unobtrusively as we could. We started heading towards the village of Milia. We walked on snow and mud, waded through a river, got pelted by driving rain and frozen by the wind as we walked through a tough forest. We were back into winter, with our heads down and pushing ahead like animals heading home; we arrived at the village of Milia, at a height of about 1,800 m, at 9:00 P.M.

With difficulty we found an inn filthier than filth. We put our covers down and took turns guarding the horses. We drank a little tea and I shared my small piece of bread and the little butter I had with the rest of them.

April 27, 1941

In the morning we succeeded in finding a couple of cups of milk. We also had some tea with some sugar that I had. We will try to go through Krania to Sitovo [Sitara], where we hope to find some food and a place to sleep for the night. Perhaps I can go to Katerini, and from there to Katahas, where I can change my clothes. We parted from Karamoshos in Krania. We will part with the rest when we get closer to Katerini. Now it is 10:00 A.M. and we will take our picture with our host Demetrios Bartjokas. Then we will get moving.

Time: 9:00 P.M.

This afternoon was the worst day of the whole expedition, because of the upsetting and vexing experience I had:

In Krania we parted with Karamoshos, because he was going towards Kryoneri, and with Tsoglanides, because he wanted to go towards Kilkis. Syropoulos wanted to stay with me and follow along the same path, so I did not look for another companion. We wanted to eat in the Krania village restaurant, although they had no luxuries, such as bread. However, the Germans had arrived there first and had searched some of the soldiers and had taken some of the mules. So, I decided to camp outside the village and sent Syropoulos to fill the mess tin with food. He filled it with lentils and we ate together. We started off and after 2 km he began complaining about the direction I was going. He said that he was worried because no one else was taking that path. For a while I calmed him down but he continued to complain. I told him he did not have to follow me and he could leave. He agreed, and he took his pack and I began walking away. I hadn't gone more than ten steps when I heard him calling me. I walked back to see what he wanted and then he asked me to give him one of my mules.

I just could not believe it when he started telling me that I had shown special preference toward my other nurse, Karamoshos, and had given him a mule and that I had never appreciated Syropoulos' work, and other stupid things like that. It looked as if we were going to have a fistfight—then he produced the gun. Suddenly I thought of my wife, my home, my dream. I had come so close from so far ... I had to reconnect myself, so I had to yield and tell him to take the mule. But he had the audacity to demand the one I was riding. Just as I was getting ready to do something risky, two young boys showed up walking toward us on the path. Happily and miraculously I came to my senses, unloaded my things and gave him the mule. As he parted he had the impudence to tell me that he will write to me and come and visit me. I forbade him to do that. He was a jerk, an ungrateful peasant, a boor.

One of the boys was going to Sitara, and I followed with my remaining mule. He guided me through a mountain path, crossing the river 15 times. I took my first bath in this river wearing my boots. In Sitara we found his grandfather Mr. Yiannouli Zisi, who was 80 years old.

In Sitara I also found a little bread and some fabulous yogurt and four eggs. Now I spread my blankets and I am getting ready to lie down. My host is very poor; he has practically nothing, but he is a very good old man. I have to give him something. I hope I can get some rest and tomorrow, after I shave, I will start for Majuria. My wife will be expecting me with great anxiety, if she is still in Thessaloniki. In any case I hope that within three days I will be in Katahas.

April 28, 1941
(Six whole months have passed since the day of my mobilization.)

In the morning I started with my guide, Christos, towards Bazouria [Paliouria]. I first examined a few patients and wrote my first post-war prescriptions. We walked all day and finally, towards sunset, we arrived in the house of Nicolas. I ate meat, the first time in ten days. I had fried pork and eggs and excellent wheat bread. The village is rich in pork and wheat. Along the way I took pictures of the monastery of St. Nicolas.

April 29, 1941

As soon as I got up I looked for a guide to take me to St. Demetrios of Katerini, but I was unsuccessful so I kept Christos, who took me up to Elati. After that I walked on my own towards Livadero. I got very tired because I was on foot—so tired that, as soon as I got to the village, I practically collapsed. I asked the mayor if someone could find me a guide. No guide was found, and no one offered to take me in as their guest except one very poor guy, Antonis. He took my mule and guided me to his house, where he and his nephew offered me the best hospitality.

Here, again, I examined a few patients. I was planning to try to put on civilian clothes and leave my military ones with Antonis. But, after talking with the teacher from the town of Servia who happened to be visiting in this town, I decided to go to Servia with all my military clothes and things.

April 30, 1941

I rested well. Now I can walk again, and I hope that in Servia I can find transportation by car. Around 10:00 A.M. we started from Livadero with the family of the teacher, Sokratis Gouras. Antonis gave me a horse for the trip for 150 dr., so with my mule loaded, myself on horseback and with the teacher's family along, I felt very safe. I hoped that soon I would arrive in Thessaloniki and see my Chrysoula. I gave all my dirty military clothes to Antonis and only kept the ones I had on. I also gave him a blanket and my tent. I will always be indebted to him for taking care of me.

It took us six hours to get to Servia. We avoided the roads where the German motorized convoys were passing. When we got to the village (a beautiful big village with walls and Byzantine churches) I saw many houses that had been destroyed by bombing. Some people left before the bombing, and their houses had been looted of all their supplies like flour, oil, butter, etc. Some people paid for their neighbors' absence. We can't really blame only the Germans, because many houses had been looted by the people next door.

I thought of leaving all my things at the teacher's house and sort of hoped that he might find me some civilian clothes. That did not happen, but I did spend the night at his house. His mother and sister-in-law who were from Thessaloniki were staying there temporarily as well. I am obliged to him for helping me out and for being my host.

May 1, 1941

It is May Day and still I'm away from home. Since this morning, I've been trying to make arrangements for my trip. I decided to leave my blanket and bedding and all my medical tools and first-aid sack, as well as other things including my camera, at the teacher's house. His sister-in-law promised to bring them to Thessaloniki, and I promised to take care of things that they had in a storage place in Athens, through my mother.

I said my goodbyes and left.

On the highway at around noon I got a ride in a German military truck, just as a simple soldier. They took me to the intersection of the road of Kozani-Veria. From there, after a long wait and a small argument with a stupid Greek lieutenant, I went to Kozani. I hoped that from there I could get to Thessaloniki by bus, which I had learned was running at the cost of 500 dr.

There I looked for the house of the lawyer Ioannis [Yannis] Goras, who was my host for that night. He is a splendid and very progressive young man.

May 2, 1941

In the morning I went with Yannis to check out the bus situation. I was lucky, because they were fixing the bus and were planning to leave at noon. Yannis suggested that I change to civilian clothes and he provided me with some. I left my military clothes with him and all of my wife's postcards that had my military address. I put the contents of my military pack in an orange sack provided by the bus. Along the way we saw many convoys of Greek soldiers going home. Rumor had it that the Germans would arrest them and use them for forced labor. On the bus no one was wearing military clothes, although, except for three women and a young girl, they were all soldiers and most probably officers.

We are slowly coming closer to the Sanatorium. It almost seems unreal that I'm here, and I will see my wife soon.

Life here appears to have retained its regular pace, despite the presence of Germans and German vehicles.

I took the tram from Egnatia and got off at Venizelou. I bought flowers and sweets. Along the way I saw people I knew who reassured me that my house was not one of those that had been confiscated by the Germans. Despite that, my yearning and fear were squeezing my heart.

I approached the complex of the two houses, my father-in-law's and ours, from the back, from the side of the small apartment building that is behind it. I saw light in one of the windows in my father-in-law's house. As I got closer, I saw a lot of light in the living room and men's shadows, and I realized the Germans were in there. It was dark and nobody saw me. I thought that perhaps they had taken only my in-laws' house. I crept around the garden and tried to look into the windows of my kitchen; I saw shirtless Germans cooking in the kitchen. Numb, and with flowers and sweets in hand, I slithered away towards the park. There I ran into the young daughter of my neighbor Hainoglou. She told me that Chrysoula and my aunt-in-law were at the Damoris' house. When I went there looking for them, I learned that the Germans had assigned the Paraskevopoulos house to Chrysoula.

At that house finally I found my aunt-in-law, who told me that Chrysoula had gone to my friend Evnouhides to get news about me,

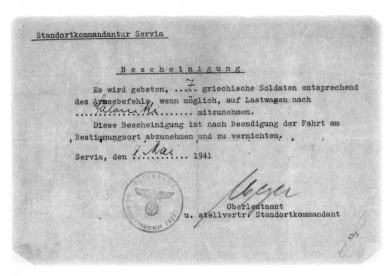

This certificate, dated May 1, 1941, authorizes transportation. It reads: "It is requested that 7 Greek soldiers according to army command be taken, if possible by truck, to Saloniki. This certificate is to be taken back at the end of the trip once it reaches final destination and is to be destroyed." It is signed by a first lieutenant and base commander.

since her husband had returned from the front before me. My aunt-in-law and Chrysoula had just returned from the island of Skiathos where they had gone with the rest of the family, fleeing the Germans. I waited for about an hour. Twice my aunt-in-law went out looking for her. Meanwhile before she had returned, I heard my Chrysoula's voice talking outside with some friends. I waited in the sitting room, and before she got in I spoke to her softly so I would not scare her.

Our emotion and excitement were so great, we were breathless. For six months I have lived for this moment, I have survived for this moment! I'm so glad to be alive!

After my sweet wife, who withstood so much, attended me, and after I bathed and changed, we had something to eat and talked about small things.

Then we lay down in bed without sleeping and talked, hugged, kissed, loved, endlessly, nonstop.

Oh, the power of the touch, the energizing flame that comes

from the closeness of two souls, the healing magic of the caress—
what difficulties can't they overcome, what miseries can't they erase!
The touch, or the embrace is not much mentioned in medical books,
but it is man's amazing gift, for healing each other. Man needs this
warmth, this touch, this love, and it is a newfound weapon for my
practice.

May 3, 1941

No time to waste; I had to get moving, so by 10:00 A.M. I was in
town to arrange all my affairs and go to the headquarters of the
National Health Insurance. Starting Monday I go to work. I called
Lazarides, did some shopping, then went home and spent the rest
of the day with my Chrysoula.

My darling, she is so tired, so psychologically shaken, from all
these adventures and especially because our nest has been taken by
the Germans. Now, however, next to me she will find her strength
and regain her powers. I will have her rest and lighten up the load
of her responsibilities. I will make her the happiest woman in the
world. We will start our new life together with new plans.

May 4, 1941

This afternoon I'm expecting the interpreter to come so I can visit
the Germans. I hope that very soon they will free up our house and
return it to us. Yesterday the German officer in charge paid us a
visit. I don't feel too comfortable with these Germans.

So, here I am, sort of like the hero of a novel with a happy ending; but is this really the ending? I'm left to wonder about the final
outcome of our tormented expedition. Will life ever be the same after I have died so many deaths, and after seeing comrades and com-
panions die? Will life ever be the same under these invaders? Will
they rape our women, slaughter us all and turn our city into rubble?
As I look at the whole picture of who I am and why I'm here, will my
only contribution be as a part of another archeological layer of this
poor Hellenic homeland that can never escape the invaders?

I'm left to wonder if there is a reason, a purpose or a lesson in what is happening, or if all life is just random ... This thought would not take root in a religious mind. Here is where religion helps; but lacking that, these thoughts cannot be allowed to overwhelm me. I have to think of the positive things that happened, the people I saved or just helped, and those who have given to me out of the goodness of their hearts.

From tomorrow I start the new battle of Life, and I will overcome all its hardships, the same way I overcame the hardships at the front. This time I will have my Chrysoula at my side and we will survive, float and sail to new seas and new horizons.

I've been away from my sweet wife for too long; to be exact: six months and four days. So my adventure comes to an end with the beginning of our new life.

From this war adventure, and these hardships, I learned the great worth of Life and Happiness.

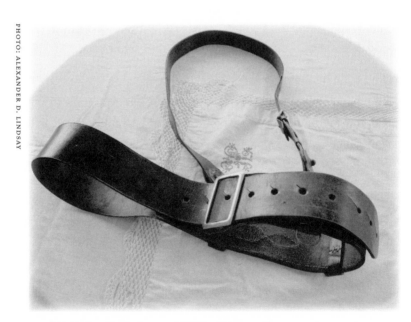

Dr. Electris wore this belt as part of his officer's uniform.

Epilogue

The Greek-Italian war and the subsequent German invasion of Greece is a small but important chapter in the overall history of World War II. The consequences of Greece's involvement in WWII are still debated. By June 1941 there was a "virtual turn in the war to the detriment of the Axis powers."[35] Some historians claim this was due in large part to Germany's failure to capitalize on its Balkan victories by not expanding its offensive to dominate the entire Mediterranean and the Middle East. But there is little doubt that the Greek-Italian war and the subsequent invasion of the Balkans by Germany contributed to the ultimate defeat of Hitler.

The invasion of Greece had a negative impact on other German campaigns. Most importantly, Hitler's invasion of Yugoslavia and Greece delayed the offensive against Russia, Operation Barbarossa, by at least four to five weeks. Some historians, especially German revisionists, vigorously contest the importance that the "four-to five-week delay" had on the outcome of the war. Others argue that the delay of Barbarossa was only caused by the severity of the Polish and Russian winter, considered one of the worst winters in recorded history. However, the voices of those present and fighting the war at that time should be given precedence. Hitler (and his generals) stated that the conquest of Yugoslavia and Greece delayed Operation Barbarossa by four to five weeks.[36] As Hitler said to Martin Bormann: "Without the Italians and the problems they caused with their idiotic campaign in Greece, I would in fact have attacked the Russians several weeks earlier."[37]

---

35 Magenheimer, p. 71.
36 Blau, p. 52.
37 Magenheimer, p. 82.

In an interchange of telegrams with Churchill, Roosevelt wrote: "You have done not only heroic but very useful work in Greece, and the territorial loss is more than compensated for by the necessity for enormous German concentration and resulting enormous German losses in men and material. Having sent all men and equipment to Greece you could possibly spare, you have fought a wholly justified delaying action ..."[38]

"As a consequence, despite the mauling they suffered in June and early July, the Russians were able to check the Wehrmacht at Smolensk, hold them at Moscow and then drive them backward into the bitter Russian winter. Had Hitler not run up a swastika on the Acropolis, he might have succeeded in draping it upon the Kremlin."[39]

"In the light of the gigantic struggle that was to begin a few weeks after their conclusion, the campaigns in the Balkans may be considered as the Wehrmacht's last blitz victories before the Germans met their fate in Russia."[40]

The Axis involvement in the Balkans and Greece was influential in other important ways in the subsequent course of WWII. To start with, it opened another front several months before the attack on Russia began, increasing the Axis powers' area of exposure. The Resistance fighting in the Balkan front became a liability for the Axis. The invasion itself was hastily executed and the Yugoslavs and Greeks were not completely disarmed. Also, before Barbarossa, the Axis had to expend a lot of energy and resources in redeploying and refitting their troops back in Germany. They had to redeploy all but three of the ground units that invaded the Balkans, as well as their Air Corps and flying units. This had to be accomplished before complete victories were realized and gains were consolidated in the Balkans.[41] Furthermore, the overwhelming speed and success of the Balkan campaign may well have made Germany overconfident and reckless in its subsequent operations.

---

38 Churchill, Vol. III, p. 208.
39 Sulzberger, p. 53.
40 Blau, p. 148.
41 Blau, p. 145.

Moreover, the Greek stance against the Italian and German invasions and the British effort to stand with the Greeks helped sway US public opinion in favor of the war. It was easier for the US government to support British operations and made the United States more inclined to be involved in the war.

The German conquest of Crete became the graveyard of the Luftwaffe; it made Hitler less confident in using it for subsequent air campaigns. As Churchill claimed, "Goering gained only a Pyrrhic victory in Crete." In addition, the British and Americans learned from Crete that parachutists should not be launched directly onto the enemy position but should land behind their objective and, once consolidated, move against the enemy.[42] They used this knowledge in their great parachute attacks in Sicily and Normandy.

My family told me the history of WWII as it happened to them as first-hand participants and eyewitnesses. It is their view of the war and the world that I am presenting—the story of people who remained optimistic in the face of all futility. They dared to dream, plan and believe that their lives could make a difference despite the Great Powers' schemes and plans of conquest.

Many Americans are amazed when I tell them that Greece even took part in WWII. To Americans, WWII is Pearl Harbor, the invasion at Normandy and the liberation of Italy and Paris. They never experienced a Blitzkrieg invasion or lived amid the devastation of an occupation. Misha Glenny, in his book *The Balkans*, describes the Blitzkrieg attack on Greece:

"Everywhere on the evening of 27 February 1941 German military teleprinters spat out one word: 'Heerestrabe,' Army Road. The starting gun for the Balkan campaign had been fired. Within hours, pontoon bridges appeared across the Danube, linking Romania with Bulgaria. Infantrymen squeezed themselves into transports and trains. On 1 March, an unending phalanx of armored cars, tanks, gun carriages, anti-aircraft equipment and horses began to roll past the Bulgarian peasants in their fields as the most ruthlessly efficient and best equipped army in history crunched its way across the Bal-

---

42 Keegan, p. 172.

kan mountain range towards the Greek-Bulgarian border and the fortified defenses of the Metaxas Line" (471).

The Germans divided Greece among themselves, the Bulgarians and the Italians. The Bulgarian occupation was cruel and aimed to eliminate all Greek elements from Thrace. They implemented ruthless "ethnic cleansing" policies and drove more than one hundred thousand Greeks from their homes and towards the western cities.[43]

The Germans were even more brutal. They drained Greece of all its resources—from plundering artworks, to mining ores, to es-

---

43 This resulted in the overcrowding of cities, which urgently had to deal with the new refugees. Hasty and ill-constructed housing of that era is still evident in the unsightly architecture of today's cities.

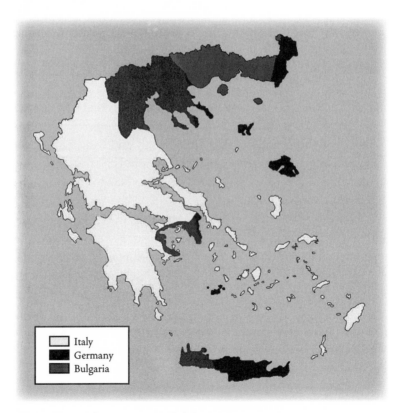

The occupation of Greece was divided three ways.

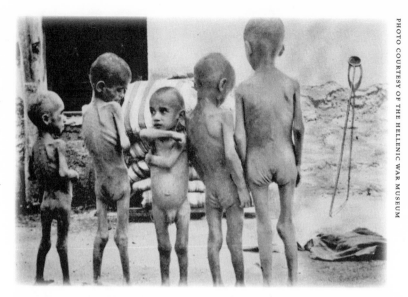

Children during the Athens famine in the winter of 1941.

sential food supplies. It was part of Hitler's *Vergeltungsmabnahme* (retaliation measures) against Greece. The Wehrmacht needed to feed and sustain its troops that had come to Greece ill-equipped, as well as supply Rommel's campaign in Africa. Besides military materials, they confiscated medicines, fuel, clothing and all forms of transportation. The Sonderkommando economic advisors who arrived in Greece were determined to strip anything of economic value from the country. They even tried to recruit laborers for Germany. When that proved difficult, they would arrest men and take them to forced labor camps in Germany. In turn the Greek farmers hid their produce. Prices began to rise and there were huge food shortages. In the winter of 1941 a famine swept through Greece, especially Athens. The situation was made worse by the severe winter and the allied blockade of Greek ports. Finally, by August of 1942, humanitarian efforts prevailed and food deliveries began arriving in Greece. The international Red Cross sent them on the Turkish ship *Kourtoulous*. The Red Cross put the number of dead in the famine of 1941–43 to be about two hundred fifty thousand. The BBC's figure was five hundred thousand.

PHOTO COURTESY OF THE HELLENIC WAR MUSEUM

To solve cash shortage problems, the Germans initiated an inflationary printing of money, thus devaluing the Greek drachma. Hyperinflation resulted, and black marketers and profiteers preyed on the common man. These actions were catastrophic for the people of Greece. When the Germans invaded, Greek government officials were the first to be evacuated to Crete. Then, they fled into exile in Egypt, thus becoming estranged from their people. The government established in Athens by the Axis was impotent and unable to take care of the people. In 1942 the Resistance movement began to form, first among the youth in the cities and then in organized groups in the mountains and in the country. The Communist Party of Greece dominated the EAM (National Liberation Front) and ELAS (National Peoples Liberation Army). The EDES (National Republican Greek League) was right wing. The SOE (British Special Operations Executive) collaborated and supported EAM/ELAS and EDES. One of the success stories of the Resistance/SOE collaboration was the destruction of the famous Gorgopotamos Bridge in November 1942. It split Greek transport in two and ended the supply lines for Rommel's campaign in Africa.

The Wehrmacht and Schutzstaffel (SS) carried out mass executions of Greek civilians as retribution to the Resistance. These reprisal policies included the increasing use of violence and terror. This was the Third Reich's military justice, as dictated by the Führer and implemented in the rest of Eastern Europe. They started by taking hostages and then randomly executing selected Greeks. Killing fifty Greeks for every dead German became the standard. Other operations ordered by General Kurt Student included "shootings, forced levies, the burning of villages, and extermination (*Austrottung*) of the male population of an entire region. In Student's words: 'All operations are to be carried out with great speed, leaving aside all formalities and certainly dispensing with special courts ... These are not meant for beasts and murderers.'

"Greek sources estimate that two thousand civilians were shot on Crete in 1941. This figure is probably exaggerated, but we do know that the village of Kandanos was razed as a warning, and that large numbers of villagers were summarily shot, not only in Kon-

The German occupation resulted in 5,000 executions.

domari but also in Alikianos and elsewhere."[44] (The men of Kondomari were shot in the olive groves outside their village on June 2, 1941.)

These massacres were repeated multiple times throughout Greece during the years of occupation. One of the worst occurred in the town of Kalavryta, where the entire male population of five hundred was killed. In 1944, it was reported to the Greek government in exile that the Germans had destroyed 879 villages completely and 460 partially.[45] The German operations against the Resistance terrorized these villagers until they departed in 1944.

The greatest tragedy of the war was the destruction of the Greek-Jewish population. From Thessaloniki alone, about fifty thousand Greek Jews were sent to the death camp at Auschwitz as part of Hitler's Final Solution. There was practically no anti-Semitism in Greece itself, most Greek Jews considered themselves Greek despite petty prejudices and hostilities of everyday life.[46] In 1941, Alfred

---

44 Mazower, p. 173.

45 Mazower, p. 183.

46 Mazower, p. 257.

Rosenberg, the commander of Souder Commando, proclaimed, "For the average Greek there is no Jewish Question. He doesn't see the political danger of a world Jewry."

The Greeks tried to save their fellow citizens and the Jews found help among all quarters of the population, especially from the Resistance fighters.

The German occupation merged seamlessly with an internal civil war (1944–1949) that left the country in ruins. In the four decades that followed WWII, Greece was also the frontline of the huge geopolitical struggle commonly known as the Cold War. Continuous interference of outside forces in Greek internal affairs created a mercurial political scene that included everything from right wing military juntas to socialist left wing governments. Ironically, Italy, the Axis country that my father fought against, escaped most of the post-WWII upheaval. Not only was its Axis involvement quickly forgiven, but it was also given much post war aid. The sad fact was that Greece ended up as the eye of the Cold War storm, while Italy was allowed to rebuild.

...

It is through the stories of Thessaloniki that the suffering of the Greeks becomes real.

The Greece of the 1940s was very different from the Greece of today. At that time, there was a huge gap between the Greece of the mountains and that of the cities. The Greece of the mountains had not caught up with the twentieth century. There were no paved roads, electricity or telephones. The villagers held to their old ways, unchanged since the times of the Turkish occupation. In some places a woman was considered little more than a beast of burden.

In contrast, the Greece of the cities, including Thessaloniki, was filled with newly arrived refugees from Asia Minor. The Asia Minor Destruction, coupled with the world depression of the 1930s, destabilized the political and economic situation in Greece. The result was a politically charged Greece, which, at the outbreak of WWII, was governed by a military dictatorship.

Before WWII, my home city of Thessaloniki (commonly called

Saloniki) was full of coffee shops, drawing rooms and restaurants with small orchestras and dance floors. There the upper and middle bourgeoisie would gather to forget their troubles, the high cost of living, the unemployment and the harassment of the Metaxas dictatorship. There was also, of course, the anguish of the impending war, with constant news of other European countries falling to the expanding power of Germany.

Saloniki was a wonderful mix of people, including Jews, Armenians and Italians. Many of the Jews were highly assimilated. The majority were Sephardic Jews, who had come from Spain following their expulsion in 1492.[47] The Jewish presence kept business and commerce vibrant in Thessaloniki and made the city more cosmopolitan. The city was also bohemian, home to many left-leaning intellectuals, artists and musicians.

However, all was changing as the first waves of WWII broke upon the Greek shores. Hostilities erupted against Italians in the city. In February 1940 Piero Arigoni, the famous Italian architect responsible for many city landmarks (like Villa Bianca, the railroad station and the electrical service building), was found murdered in his home. Many people of mixed Italian and Greek parentage disowned even their own parents. It became evident that cultural tensions were stirring in Greece.

By the winter of 1940–41 Greece and Thessaloniki were totally engulfed in war. The sounds of sirens and bombs falling, followed by people running to shelters, became part of everyday life.[48]

Residents never forgot that particular Wednesday, the 9th of

---

47 In 1492 the Alhambra Decree, signed by Ferdinand and Isabella, expelled all the Jews from Spain. This was due to a combination of Catholic religious zeal and prejudice. Many of them were allowed to settle in the city of Thessaloniki, which had come under the Ottoman rule after the fall of the Byzantium in 1453. The city was depopulated by the Turks. Most of the city's Byzantine residents, artisans and merchants had been slaughtered or sold into slavery. Thus, the Turks needed people to restart the economy of the old port.

48 Even my present home in Thessaloniki still bears the marks of the Italian bomb that fell in January of 1941. The bombs were aiming to destroy the nearby military hospital.

April, when the Germans marched to the entrance of Thessaloniki, Vardaris Square, and the archbishop, the mayor and the military commander gave the keys of the city to German commander Von List.

My Aunt Elli claims that the Greek resistance started on the 27th of April, when the young Greek who was forced to raise the Nazi flag on the Acropolis jumped off the Acropolis rock and committed suicide.

The Germans had expropriated the house my mother and father built as newlyweds to use as part of their headquarters. When my mother got the house back (see Aunt Elli's story at the end of the epilogue), everything had been ransacked. The Germans stole art, rugs, silver and other valuables and heirlooms. The pillows were ripped and even her childhood porcelain dolls were sliced open and thrown on the terrace. Everything in my childhood home had a German fingerprint or footprint, from the broken locks on the furniture to the pockmarks on the floor left by Nazi boots. (Those pockmarks were convenient stopping points for the marble games my brother and I used to play.)

Our neighborhood back then was called the "neighborhood of journalists." Just about everyone was either a journalist or a writer. They were all to one degree or another involved with the Resistance. The Germans had seized the city radio station and turned it into the major Nazi propaganda station in southeastern Europe. They shut down all the newspapers except two. One of them, *Nea Evropi* (New Europe), became their official propaganda paper. Arrests and executions routinely appeared there along with many anti-Semitic articles. All radios were forbidden and confiscated. In our old house there were remnants of the hiding places for the radio during the occupation.

The war affected all members of our family. My mother's brother ended up in Egypt fighting alongside the British. My mother's sister's fiancé was taken to a German forced labor camp; he did not return to Greece, nor did anyone hear from him, for six years. She married someone else, and always felt sad about it. My father's sister died during the war and the husband of his other sister was killed during the civil war.

Transportation was disrupted in the city and food supplies confiscated by Germans. My aunt recalls one day in July of 1941 when it was announced that there would be no bread available in the bakeries. The famine started soon thereafter. The endless soup lines were comprised of the elderly, disabled war veterans and skin-and-bone children. Desperately hungry people scavenged through German garbage cans. People died in the streets and were buried without coffins and the services of priests. In the area of Kalamaria, one of the poorest in Thessaloniki, many diseases killed hundreds of people. My father often saw children with huge boils and deformities due to vitamin deficiencies.

Many Greeks came to believe that the Germans were implementing systematic extermination of the population through starvation. That turned out not to be true; the Germans consumed all the food and had no interest in the plight of the Greeks.

Inflation was so bad that a loaf of bread costing ten drachmas in April 1941 cost 1,500 drachmas by the summer of '42, and much more in the years that followed. The national economy collapsed and inflation, coupled with black-marketeering, became the status quo.

These Axis policies created a chaotic, destructive governing structure in Greece between 1941–44. The government put in place by the Germans and the Italians was weak and completely unable to help the citizens, especially those in Thessaloniki. In order to survive, people banded together and many of them became radicalized. In the Greece of the mountains, a surrogate state was beginning to form, dominated by the left wing resistance groups EAM/ELAS. These leftist groups were immensely popular and held an almost mystical connection with underground groups in Thessaloniki. The mountain and city groups shared common dreams and goals.

Sabotage by resistance groups resulted in arrests, executions and terror. On the hottest day in July of 1941, all the Jewish males of the city were corralled into Eleftheria Square and subjected to the most inhumane treatment. Many people my family knew died that day. The Germans created ghettos and concentration camps throughout the city. Lines of people—women with children, the elderly and war veterans—were marched along Egnatia Street to some camp or another. From there they were loaded on trains for a trip with no return.

My mother told me that one of the worst days in her life was the day she was passing the square by the front of the railroad station. The Germans had gathered Jewish people for deportation. They had split up interfaith families, leaving out the non-Jewish members. My mother remembered the cries, cries that she never forgot until the end of her life. She felt as if there were a hum hanging over the whole city of Thessaloniki.

One summer day in 1942 my mother felt like her life was over. A German officer grabbed my brother Paul from his stroller while my mother walked him along a road near the sea. She always made a special effort to stay away from areas that were frequented by the Germans. She never saw this officer coming until he stopped her and lifted my brother from the stroller. My terrified mother kneeled down in the middle of the street, embraced the baby stroller and started crying. She remained there for an indeterminate amount of time, unable to think or do anything. At some point the officer came back, accompanied by another soldier, carrying candy and canned milk. They were kissing my brother, who would not stop crying.

The officer told my mother, in French, that my brother was a beautiful "German baby," since he was very blond and had blue eyes (just like my father). He told her that his wife back home had a baby about my brother's age and that he had not seen him. He invited my mother to come and visit him at the headquarters any time. My mother was speechless—she grabbed her baby and ran.

She never again took my brother out for a stroll until the Germans departed.

Another barbarous deed committed by the Germans was the destruction of the ancient Jewish cemetery. In collaboration with a few Greek workmen, the Germans turned the cemetery into a quarry of tombstones, which were used later for building materials by both Germans and Greeks. The cemetery area is where the Aristotelian University has since been built.

That was only the beginning of the "passion" of the Thessaloniki Jews. My aunt's classmate, Morris, was saved by joining the Resistance in the mountains. Other Jewish friends found their way to

Athens where they lost themselves in anonymity. By August 1943 Thessaloniki had almost been emptied of its Jews.

During the last years of the occupation most people in Thessaloniki lived in complete terror of the Gestapo and the Greek military Security Battalions (*Tagmatasfalites*), who collaborated with the Germans and searched for any and all they considered part of the Resistance. Our neighborhood of journalists was always under a raid or a blockade.

My aunt told me how she warned the mother of a young friend that a blockade was being set up, and her friend must escape. By revealing this information, she put herself and our whole family in danger. A few hours later she witnessed from behind the drapes her friend's mother being beaten by the military police. Her friend had escaped.

The area of Kalamaria, where many of my father's patients lived, was frequently singled out by the military police. On an August day in 1943, the Gestapo and the military police surrounded and killed many people who they considered "communists." They murdered them in front of their families—mothers, brothers, children.

There were terrifying times when even my father was interrogated. He had a special pass as a doctor that allowed him to move around the city at night. I may never know if my father was a member of the Resistance. I know, though, that his sympathies were with his patients, who struggled with inflation, hunger, black marketers, disease, desperation resulting from the collapse of their country, and, most of all, terror. His sympathies saw no political affiliations. As a matter of fact, he began to despise the politicizing of the Resistance movements because he saw its divisiveness.

The day of the Allied landing in Normandy, the SS gathered one hundred Thessaloniki hostages from the Pavlos Melas camp and executed them outside the city on the road to Kilkis. The Gestapo, in collaboration with the Military Security Battalions, burned alive 170 villagers from Hortiati in the village bakery as a reprisal for the killing of one German soldier. Aside from their deportation and subsequent extermination of the Jews, this was the biggest crime that the Axis and their collaborators committed in the area of Thessaloniki.

In September of 1944 American planes began bombing Thessaloniki. They bombed the storage warehouses in the port and in the Ladadika area. The next day many people, ignoring the SS and the military police, looted the bombed warehouses and celebrated.

On October 30, 1944, the Wehrmacht departed. As they exited they tried to blow up the electrical plant on St. Demetrios Street. They were stopped by an EAM/ELAS group.

The Greeks did not have much time to celebrate the end of the German occupation, because the civil war that followed was worse in many ways. At that time Greece had three governments: the Nazi-influenced government in Athens, the British-influenced government of the King in exile and the temporary National Independence Movement government in the mountains.

Clashes between nationalist and left wing guerilla groups had started even before the Germans departed. As of February 4, 1944, in Yalta, Stalin had already accepted that Greece would be under the British sphere of influence. However, this fact remained unknown to the partisans and guerillas of the EAM/ELAS. These groups believed in an idealistic communist dream, and on December 3, 1944, the country was dragged in the bloody civil war.

The Greek poet Yiannis Ritsos eloquently wrote of the war:

Oh! Yes, yes so many stupid battles, heroic sacrifices and losses
  And more battles afterwards for things,
    That already had been decided by others....

Some of my parents' friends and relatives, the intellectuals, moderates and idealists, had the bad judgment to be persuaded by professional party Communists to join the group. It was bizarre that the *crème de la crème* of the Greek intellectuals allowed the worst and most ruthless Communist Party members to be their mouthpiece. There was great confusion as to who held what political beliefs. Innocent people were viewed as traitors, some murdered by the left, others imprisoned and killed by the right. During the civil war many Greek people were concerned that the communist empire plans of Tito and Stalin would swallow Greece.

I never knew about these horrible times until I was in high school. My mother explained that she and my father believed that the logic of violence and terror that tore Greece apart was deeply rooted in the Axis strategies during the occupation. My family did not starve during the German occupation because my father was always in great demand as a doctor and paid in kind. Much of the family's gold went towards the purchase of food. My childhood was made safe by the silences people kept about the horrors that had passed.

When the soldiers returned from the Albanian front there were no communal rites of purification for coming home from war. There were people crippled and maimed; most experienced post-traumatic effects. WWII and the horrible civil war affected almost every one of my father's patients. Each person experienced the loss of a loved one, property or even a body part. My father worked selflessly to serve the people of eastern Thessaloniki and especially Kalamaria. He was a doctor, psychologist, confidant and life coach. He built Kalamaria's first socialized medical center, serving the surrounding area, which consisted mostly of Pontic Greek and other refugees from Asia Minor. I cannot remember a dinner party at our house that my father did not have to run out on call. The phone rang often in the middle of the night and I can still hear the hushed voices of my parents going past my bedroom door. When the city was hit by epidemics like diphtheria, my father would disappear for weeks at a time. Tuberculosis ran rampant in the post-war years and my father was one of the top diagnosticians in the field.

Several years ago, while I worked in the yard of my house in Thessaloniki, a man stopped to ask me if I knew Dr. Electris. When I said I was his daughter, the man proceeded to tell me how my father had diagnosed his tuberculosis and sent him to a sanatorium, thus saving his life. This person was a Pontic Greek from the Kalamaria area. He said that to my father all people were equal; he served both the right wing and the communists the same. He never refused medical services to anyone; he would even take care of a Nazi if necessary. His belief was that the best medicine for anyone was a tablespoon of kindness.

I already knew much of what the man was telling me. Our house was like a railroad station. There were always two or three people I did not know eating dinner with us. There were men caring for orphaned children, blind, people with amputated limbs (some of them my teachers) and old Jewish patients who had lost all their family members. Many were foreigners; some would show up again and again and others would disappear after only one visit. There were many spirited discussions and sometimes arguments around the table.

My father's kidneys never recovered from his time at the front and he died of nephritis in 1958. My mother worked as director of the Center of Social and Mental Health and created the first public school for mentally handicapped children in Thessaloniki. In 1963 she went to the United States on a Fulbright scholarship to further her training in social work and psychology.

Like most Greek cities, my parents' elegant and cultured town of Thessaloniki became crowded with people from the countryside. They searched for safe refuge from the primitive conditions and the terrifying ravages of the civil war. A large portion of Thessaloniki's bohemian, intellectual and sophisticated bourgeoisie, both Christian and Jewish, had died in German concentration camps, or were in exile in communist countries. The survivors found their lives radically changed in their struggle to find housing, raise families and avoid persecution for political beliefs. To my parents' generation it seemed that their city was devoid of its past gentility. However, they had survived WWII, the civil war and the Cold War. The mere fact that a new generation of Greeks was still left to grow up gave them hope for the future.

The Greeks themselves do not seek recognition for their contribution to WWII. Nor do they ask reparations from their previous occupiers. Now Greece, Italy and Germany are partners in the European Union. They face similar challenges in their efforts to preserve European culture and civilization. The Greeks who lived through the horrors of WWII and the civil war are dying out. However, we, and the generations to come all over the world, must never forget what happened: we must remember for the sake of peace.

How Chrysoula Got Her House Back
(as narrated by Aunt Elli to Helen Electrie Lindsay)

Our father wanted us to leave Thessaloniki. He had three daughters and was afraid of the Germans. His eyes had seen many bad things through all the wars and catastrophes ... He also had worked for the Agricultural Bank and he hoped that it would have continued its operations in Athens.

We embarked in a boat—merely a fishing caïque that was in the worst shape—with the island of Mytilini as the destination. We were in such a hurry to leave that we forgot our hunting dog in the basement; the dog barked all night long, so no one went into our house. That was a fortunate thing because there were various people looking for empty houses to break into and loot. The next day our uncle Xenophon went in and took our hunting dog, our rugs and some of our trunks that were left packed. The rest of our things were looted by the Germans.

When the boat was pulling out of the port, we were leaving a burning city. Thessaloniki was burning. All the storehouses and warehouses with supplies and gasoline tanks exploded and burned. It felt as if we had a tourniquet around our hearts that was tightening and tightening ... History was repeating itself again. We were losing our second country, our homes, and what we had saved when we restarted our lives from scratch after the Asia Minor Destruction. Were our new roots, which were just beginning to take hold, going to be cut off again?

Our trip was horrid; we were in a terrible storm, a tempest with huge waves. We all were seasick, and were certain that we would drown. The captain was finding it impossible to sail towards Mytilini; he was blown in the opposite direction, so he tried to get to the island of Skiathos.

I will forever remember the dreamy sight of the island of Skiathos. The sea was like glass. The menacing waves had fallen; we were out of the storm. At that moment our new shelter was a gift from God.

Our father found us a house near the port and then he left in a hurry for Athens to look for our brother Nikos. We had received news that the front had been broken and the retreat of our troops had started. I was actually having a good time, was not taking things too seriously and looking at it as a great adventure; after all it was spring in Skiathos. Your mother, on the other hand, was going through some extreme agony. She was feeling bad for leaving and was worried that Phaedia would get to Thessaloniki and not find her. She was tortured by guilty feelings for her desertion ...

Meanwhile, perhaps for diversion, or to make up for her bad feelings, she started working with the mayor of the village. They were trying to help the English, who were coming down from the front to find passage on boats and caïques to Egypt and the Middle East.

We learned that the Germans were coming to Skiathos the next day. Your mother was told that she might be in danger for helping the English. Also her longing for Phaedia, and her fright that he would return home and not find her, made her decide to take Thia [Aunt] Mahi and hop on the first boat she could get that was going back to Thessaloniki. Our father was not there to stop her, or say anything ...

We, the next day, saw the Germans arriving in boats.

Those moments remain in my memory like a movie clip.

We were locked up in our houses and were peering out from the cracks in the shutters. There were two or three men standing in the harbor, fishermen, captains standing erect looking at the coming boats. They wore shabby suit jackets and buttoned up shirts, clothes they might have worn to a funeral ... Perhaps one of them was the mayor ... The Germans tried to dock their boats and were reaching out for some help. No one on the dock was moving. The Germans in the first boat made a couple of passes towards the dock. Then one of the captains who was further forward, after putting his thumb aside of his nose and blowing his nose to the ground with the characteristic gesture of a man in disgust, stretched out the same hand, gave it to the German and pulled him in.

Meanwhile, your mother was encountering another storm and tempest. The caïque that was taking them back to Thessaloniki was smaller than the one that brought us to Skiathos and it almost sank. When she got to Thessaloniki, your mother told us, she found the house occupied by the Germans. How she found the guts to walk in I do not know. All I know was that a huge German grabbed her arm and took her to the commander. He in turn asked her: "What business do you have here madam? Don't you know that you can be shot on the spot for what you have done?" Your mother, who was always very shy, miraculously maintained her calm and composure. First she answered him in French and then in English, telling him that the building that they were in was her house. Then he asked her why she was not speaking any German. Her answer was that German was the next language she was working on—your mother was always very good in diplomatic affairs. To make a long story short, she charmed him. She told him of all her efforts to have and build a house, that she was a newlywed bride of three months when her beloved husband left for the front, and that she did not know where he was. She told him, as she always does with sweetness, reciting French poetry and quoting German philosophers, of the great efforts of humans to build their homes and nests ... I would not doubt that she probably had the German commander crying.

He started telling her his life story, how he was Austrian and of equally cultured upbringing, how he was a newlywed and his wife was expecting a child, how he was forced into this war ... and how his division was going to move back to Germany for redeployment. He promised your mother that after his division moved on, she could have her house back! He also told her that he would write to her when he returned to his home in Austria. Of course she never heard from him after he had left. Most probably he left his bones in some Russian battlefield ... In the beginning the Germans were polite; they didn't want to make the Greeks mad, they knew we were a tough enemy ... That did not last though, they started committing the atrocities that they are known for ...

Well, this is the miraculous way that your mother got her house back.

Aunt Elli's Poem

This poem was written by Aunt Elli, Dr. Electris' sister in-law, and sent to him while at the front. It is supposedly written by the cat, Frifris, who calls him "Daddy." On the upper left corner of the letter there is a round seal with the word *logokrisia*, indicating that, like most correspondence, this letter was censored. The poem has a slightly satiric tone and in an oblique way it refers to some political events that were taking place in Greece at the time. The first was the anticipated alliance between Greece and Yugoslavia, which is alluded to in the third verse: the cat declares truce with the dog in order to chase away the stray cats. The second was the censorship of mail going to the front; on the fourth verse the cat censors his mistress's letter and puts his seal on it with a kiss.

My dearest Daddy I'm so glad,
To get your latest letter read
And find out with great surprise
That you can really write in rhyme.

So after deep contemplation
I'll delve in poetic experimentation.
And the answer to your letter
you'll receive
In verse indeed!

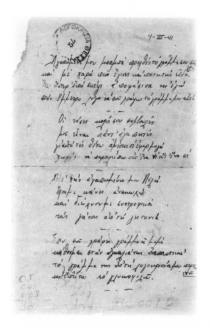

So, our dearest dog Lily,
Has signed a truce with me.
Together we chase away and scare,
All stray cats from everywhere.

When my mommy writes letters to you,
I sit on her lap and watch.
Each note I censor, but never miss
To give it a great big kiss.

I have a crazy appetite
And since they always feed me right
I have become big and strong and great.
And that is quite an awe-inspiring trait!

The only trouble, I just fear,
Is that Lent is almost nearly here;
And if it's time for mom to fast,
What food will there be for a cat?

So Daddy dearest,
As I finish now, with respect so grand,
I passionately lick your adored hand.
With hope and joy your homecoming
I await
Worthy of his dad.

Your son,
Frifris

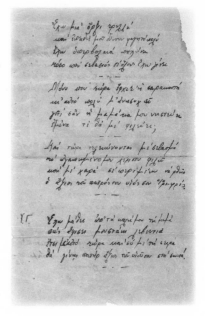

P.S.

I learned from my sweetest mom
That you have grown whiskers and
mustache.
So very appropriately you have
become,
A father worthy of his son!

Appendix

An Abridged History of Greek Involvement in World War II

Escalation

During 1939 and 1940 the Italians continuously and overtly provoked the Greeks. The Greeks in turn had been preparing defenses along their borders in Macedonia and Epirus. The threat along the Bulgarian border was not as eminent because King Boris of Bulgaria wanted to stay uninvolved until events had run their course. Greece also had a peace treaty with Turkey and Yugoslavia. However, Yugoslavia was playing a waiting game as well; it had an old peace treaty with Greece and a 1937 secret friendship pact with Bulgaria. After Italy annexed Albania in 1939, the Greeks felt threatened and turned their attention to their western borders (the Western Front), leaving only four divisions in Eastern Macedonia and Thrace (the Eastern Front).

The terms of the 1939 agreement between Greece and Great Britain required that the British assist the Greeks in the event of a military attack. In 1940 the British were immersed in their own war, fighting Germany at home and Italy in North Africa. When the Greek-Italian war began, Sir Anthony Eden, then British war minister, considered the war in Egypt and Libya more important than the Greek-Italian war. Winston Churchill, however, promised to provide all possible assistance to the Greeks in fighting a common enemy.

At the same time, the Greek government worried about provoking the Germans by inviting in British troops or setting up air bases north of Mount Olympus.

Thus the British assistance to Greece at the beginning of the war was limited. The urgency for more assistance surfaced in spring of 1941 when large concentrations of German troops in Romania threatened Greece.

The British committed to the naval defense of Greece against hostile actions of the Italian fleet. They also offered four squadrons of bombers along with the required personnel and equipment, despite the fact that there were no air bases in Greece capable of servicing modern planes. The rest of the material aid consisted of small weapons and artillery, a considerable percentage of which had been captured by the British in the war against the Italians in Libya.

The Italian-German war against Greece can be divided into six different phases:

The Italians Invade
The Greeks Fight Back
We Will Prevail (At the Western Front)
The Germans Invade
The Return Home
The Fall of Crete

The Italians Invade

The Italian army was statistically superior to the Greek forces. The Italian armies at the Albanian front amounted to two hundred forty to two hundred fifty thousand men.[49] They had been mobilized and outfitted with modern weaponry well in advance of the invasion. The Italian air force consisted of four hundred modern aircraft and a large number of trained flying personnel. The Greek army in the Albanian theatre of operations amounted to approximately 232,000 newly mobilized men. The Greeks had barely 143 planes, two-thirds of which were outdated and staffed with insufficient flying personnel. From a geographical point of view, however, the Greeks had the advantage. The mountain ranges along the Epirus and Macedonia borders form a natural defense line, and the rivers in fall and winter transform themselves into impassable torrents.

The Italian plan was to launch a surprise attack against the Greeks along the Albanian border in the Epirus and Pindos mountain areas. They planned to attack in three prongs with the intention of breaking through the Greek lines. The Greek plan was purely

---

49 *Abridged History*, p. 73.

defensive. Through general mobilization Greek troops hastily but in good order transferred to the front.

By the *12th of November* General Alexandros Papagos managed to move over one hundred infantry battalions to the front.

During the night of *November 11–12*, the British Fleet Air Arm attacked three Italian battleships in the gulf of Taranto, cutting off the supply line of the Italian troops in Albania. The British also set up air bases in Crete and Limnos threatening the Ploesti oilfields.

On the Epirus front the Greek VIII Division succeeded in holding back the Italians. In some areas the Italian superiority forced the Greeks to retreat briefly, but after receiving reinforcements the Greeks gained control.

In the Pindos sector the Greeks were forced far back. The Italian forces, attacking from the east, had reached the village of Vovousa and were threatening to envelope the Greek forces in Epirus. However, the Greeks concentrated all their troops near the mountain of Pindos and closed the gaps.

By the *13th of November* the Greek armies had regained control of the greater part of their national territories. General Papagos was determined to take advantage of the Italian mistakes before their numerical and material superiority came into play. By the *14th of November* the Greek armies went on the offense from the Ionian Sea all the way to Lake Prespa, and they threatened to capture Valona (Avlona),[50] the principal Italian supply port. In the northern section the Greeks were triumphant after a fierce battle in the Morovo-Ivan area: Greek Special Forces "K" entered the city of Corce (Koritsa) on the *22nd of November*.

The Greek troops marched at night, sometimes in mountainous terrain, under continuous Italian bombing. They experienced severe weather and struggled through shortages of food and ammunition.

The rail lines in Greece ended in the city of Florina, and all paved roads from Thessaly and Macedonia terminated at mountainsides. After the first rains the roads were rendered impassable to vehicles, and the armies sought provisions from the villagers of the Pindos

---

50 Greeks and Albanians often have different names for the same cities.

Mountains. Rationing of supplies became necessary and often even that was impossible.

The Greeks Fight Back

By December an early winter settled in, and temperatures sometimes dropped as low as $-22°$ c $(-8°$ F$)$. Snow, freezing rain, lack of appropriate clothing and supplies and a shortage of food made life almost unbearable. But the Greek troops persevered, and within a month and half they succeeded in chasing the Italians out of Greece and deep into Albania.

The Greek army lacked tanks, anti-tank weapons and motorized vehicles, so it was necessary to avoid the plains and valleys in their attacks and instead concentrate on the mountain heights. On the other side, the Italians enjoyed complete air supremacy and could escape in their motorized vehicles through the valleys, to reestablish themselves in other positions.

In the southern section of the front and along the Adriatic coast the A Army Corps crossed the Thiamis River in pursuit of the Italian army. On *December 6* they captured Agii Saranta (Sarande) and on the *8th*, Argyrokastron (Gjirokaster). Meanwhile, in the central section of the front and along the Pindos Mountains, the B Army advanced into Albania across the treacherous and lofty terrain of Gramos Mountain. By *December 5*, the B Army had captured Premeti, Fraseri (Frasher), Erseke and Leskovik. On the northern sector of the front the C and E Armies advanced over the Morova-Ivan massif and occupied the high plateau of Corce. They destroyed the 9th Italian army, capturing two thousand prisoners and taking many field weapons, machine guns and anti-tank guns.

During this period, fifteen Italian infantry divisions and one armored division were deployed on the Albanian front, arrayed against Greek defense forces that included only eleven infantry divisions, one infantry brigade and one cavalry division.

We Will Prevail (At the Western Front)

The Greeks captured Klissoura by the *10th of January* and advanced towards the heights of Trebessina. By *January 25* they had secured the line along the locations of Trebessina-Boubessi-Mali Spandarit. There they suspended operations, intending to wait out the winter. On *January 26* the Italians launched an attack in an attempt to recapture Klissoura, but the Greeks responded with strong forces, advanced, and were able to repulse the Italians. After that the Italians suspended their operations because of their heavy losses of both men and supplies. The A and B armies failed to capture Tepelene in February.

Mussolini, however, knowing that the Germans were preparing to invade Greece and hoping to atone for his defeats, prepared a huge strike against Greece, called the Primavera (Spring) Offensive. Starting at the end of December, the Italian army received reinforcements and the Greeks were suffering from battle fatigue. The Primavera attack started on *March 9* with heavy bombardment and continued undiminished until the *15th*. The brunt was borne by the Greek I, II, V, XI, XV and XVII divisions. The fighting concluded with violent hand-to-hand conflict involving the use of hand-grenades and bayonets. Height 731, which was between the Apsos and Aoos rivers, resembled Dante's *Inferno*. There were at least eighteen offensives against it, and the losses on both sides were immense.

The Primavera Offensive, however, failed completely and was abandoned by the *25th*. Mussolini, who had set himself up on one of the heights near the town of Glava to observe, left Tirana totally disappointed but planning to return.

Within a few days the British navy scored another victory against the Italians in Greek waters. The first was south of Matapan and the second off the island of Gaudo. Eight Italian ships sunk and the Italian navy ceased being a force in the eastern Mediterranean.

THE MAJOR PLAYERS

By the middle of *March 1941* the waiting game was over. King Boris of Bulgaria had committed himself to the Axis. British Intelligence was assessing what Prince Regent Paul of Yugoslavia would commit to the Axis as well. Large numbers of German troops were concentrated in Romania and were also working in Bulgaria to make infrastructural improvements needed for military operations. It was evident that Eastern Macedonia and Thessaloniki were the Germans' main objectives. British diplomats in Yugoslavia worked feverishly to overthrow the pro-German government.

Between January and March of 1941 many meetings took place between British and Greek political and military officials to best figure out how to face the German military threat. The Greeks were worried that inadequate British help would encourage the Germans to invade instead of deterring them.

During this period, on the *29th of January*, Greek Prime Minister Metaxas died and was succeeded by Alexandros Koryzis.

By *February 22* the Greek government agreed in principal to accept British military help and "rejected a German offer of immunity from invasion in return for neutrality."[51] However, all this was conditional on Yugoslavia's involvement.

"The Greeks decided to run the risk of being stabbed in the back by the Germans while holding the Italian front rather than to be defeated by both enemies simultaneously."[52]

The British Expeditionary Force began to arrive in Greece by *March 7*. It enhanced British military prestige, but it came too late and in insufficient numbers to help the Greek defense against the Germans. It was formed of various British, Australian and New Zealand units, a force of about fifty-eight thousand men. These troops, though fully motorized, were outfitted for desert warfare instead of mountainous expedition. Their anti-aircraft guns and tanks were limited. At that time the British were also defending Malta, so they had few aircraft available for Greece.

---

51 Magenheimer, p. 174.
52 Blau, p. 68.

It is important to mention that the British were not able to persuade Turkey to be involved in the Balkan defense. By *March 4*, Ismet Inonu, the Prime Minister of Turkey, and Hitler in an exchange of communications reaffirmed their friendly relations, which dated back to WWI.

Meanwhile, the Yugoslavian government of the Regent, Prince Paul, had signed the Tripartite Agreement. However, he was overthrown in a *coup d'état* on the *26th of March*. The new government in power declared a general mobilization.

That same day the British and Greeks agreed upon a strategic plan: the Greek forces were going to defend the Beles-Nestos area and combined British-Greek forces would secure the Vermio area.

Hitler, outraged with the events in Yugoslavia, launched a simultaneous attack against both Greece and Yugoslavia on *April 6th*.

Starting with the savage bombardment of Belgrade, the Germans defeated Yugoslavia in twelve days. This defeat paved the way for the invasion of Greece.

The Germans Invade

On the morning of *April 6th*, without adhering to the usual diplomatic formalities, the Germans began their invasion of Greece from the Greek-Bulgarian border at two points, and from Yugoslavia.

The German Air Force bombed and devastated the port of Piraeus. It sank six Allied ships and also bombed a British merchant ship full of explosives, triggering a huge explosion that destroyed ten other ships.

One German division, after defeating the Yugoslavians, turned south and advanced along the Axios valley, threatening to encircle the Eastern Macedonian Army as it defended the Metaxas line.

Simultaneously, other German divisions undertook the frontal attack of the Metaxas line. The Greeks defended valiantly, some of the fortifications holding on tenaciously. But one by one each fortification fell, even the strongholds, brought down only after the Germans used heavy artillery and dive-bombers. The Germans also penetrated a seven-thousand-foot, snow-covered mountain pass that was considered impassable by the Greeks and attacked the Rupel Gorge from both the south and north.[53]

By the evening of *April 9* the Germans had reached Seres. Other German divisions moved south from Bulgaria and occupied Western Thrace. It was impossible to withdraw and evacuate the Greek Eastern Macedonia Field Army because there were no ships available, and no forces to cover their withdrawal.

In order to avoid pointless sacrifice, the Eastern Macedonian Army capitulated on the *9th of April* in Thessaloniki.

The Return Home

After April 9 the Germans advanced at three points: they crossed the Axios River towards Edessa, entered Greece through Yugoslavia, and occupied Florina and seized Ahris, establishing contact with the Italians at the Western Front.

They were endangering the rear of the combined Greek and British "W" forces under General Wilson at the Vermio area. The British then decided to withdraw to the Olympus area. After fierce fighting in that area they had to retreat farther south along the axis of Larissa-Lamia-Athens.

On *April 11* the Italians marched across the Albanian border into Greece and occupied positions where the Greeks had expelled them before.

By the *12th of April*, it was decided that the Greek Northern Epirus Forces would begin withdrawal from the Albanian front and from central Macedonia to a defensive line stretching westward from Mount Olympus to the river Aliakmon, to Mount Vasilitsa and on to the Ionian Sea. They continued to fall back on the *14th*. Despite enormous difficulties, they were not defeated. They traveled moun-

---

53 A Greek colonel commanding one of the fortifications at Fort Rupel told his garrison: "We will hold them with our teeth." When the Germans overcame the fort they found written in chalk on a wall above the fallen Greeks: "At Thermopylae the three hundred were killed. Here the eighty will fall defending their country" (Sulzberger, p.52).

tain paths and crossed swollen rivers through rain and snowstorms until they finally occupied the positions they were assigned.

The Germans advanced southwards and captured Kalambaka, putting their forces between the British Expeditionary Corps and the Greek army that was retreating from Albania. The Greeks were in danger of being encircled.

By *April 16* the British-Greek defense line was collapsing. It was decided that the British would fall back to Thermopylae and hold up the Germans, in order to give the rest of their Expeditionary Corps time to evacuate Greece for Crete and Egypt. The Greek forces, unable to fall back, instead turned towards Epirus.

At the Kastoria Pass, where the Germans were trying to block the Greek retreat, heavy fighting took place between the Greeks and Germans. By the *20th* the Greek army at the Albanian front was surrounded. In order to save the Greek army from destruction or capture, several commanders and Bishop Vlahos of Ioannina asked the king and the general staff to consider surrendering to the Germans. The political and military leadership denied the request because they felt obligated to the British to support their evacuation.

The troops were demoralized, and many considered it futile to continue fighting. A telegram sent to the general staff by the commander of the B Army Corps explained the desperate situation of the troops and requested a political solution. Prime Minister Koryzis committed suicide, feeling he could not reconcile the demands of the troops with the policies of the government. Churchill called the situation "convulsive."[54]

The commander of C Army Corps, Lieutenant General G. Tsolakoglou, after communicating with the commanders of A and B corps and most division commanders, initiated surrender to the Germans on *April 20* in Votonosi, Metsovo.[55] After the capitulation the Greek Army was forced to march southward. The evacuation of the combined British, Australian, New Zealand and Polish troops

---

54 Churchill, Vol. III, p. 200.
55 *Abridged History*, p. 244.

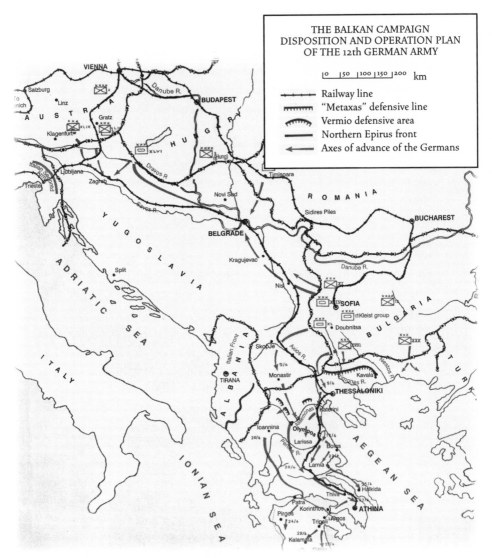

THE BALKAN CAMPAIGN
DISPOSITION AND OPERATION PLAN
OF THE 12th GERMAN ARMY

|0 |50 |100 |150 |200   km

+—+—+— Railway line
╥╥╥╥╥ "Metaxas" defensive line
⌒⌒⌒⌒ Vermio defensive area
——— Northern Epirus front
←——— Axes of advance of the Germans

See color version of this map on page 229.

from Greece was coded Operation Demon. It started on the *26th*
and lasted for six days.

To finish the evacuation, the British made a last stand at Thermopylae, abandoned on *April 25* after two days of very strong and

brave resistance. It is said that the British in Cairo secretly planned the evacuation while the troops were being transferred to Greece.[56]

It should be noted that the Greek people treated the retreating British with respect and gratitude: "Unlike the Belgians and the French, they were not inclined to blame the British for their disasters; they cheered the weary British soldiers driving off to the south."[57]

At least eighty percent of the British forces were evacuated from eight small southern ports. This was made possible with the help of Royal and Greek Navies. Twenty-six ships, twenty-one of which were Greek, were destroyed by air bombardment. Following that, Churchill wrote, "the small but efficient Greek Navy now passed under British control ... Thereafter, the Greek Navy was represented with distinction in many of our operations in the Mediterranean."[58]

The initial truce signed by Georgios Tsolakoglou on *April 20* had honorable terms and, under strict orders from Hitler, it was kept secret from the Italians. The Greek forces were obliged to withdraw to the old Greek-Albanian border within ten days and to demobilize and return home. The officers were allowed to keep their weapons and were not considered prisoners of war. The Germans, however, failed to keep their promises. Even as negotiations were being conducted, they were savagely bombarding Ioannina, and the next day they violated the agreement. The Italians also began a series of attacks and bombardments that caused great losses. The Germans forced Tsolakoglou to sign a new agreement, this time as a prisoner of war. The terms were worse and the officers were considered prisoners of war. The Greeks would be forced to capitulate to the Italians as well.

On the *23rd of April*, Tsolakoglou was humiliated again when he was taken to Thessaloniki to sign a third protocol. The "capitulation agreement" was the unconditional surrender of the Greek army to both the Axis powers. The carriage road of Igoumenitsa-Bisdouni-

---

56   Blau, p. 113.
57   Lukacs, p. 130.
58   Churchill, Vol. III, p. 206.

Metsovo was a designated line of demarcation; Greek soldiers north of the line were prisoners of the Italians, and those south of that line prisoners of the Germans.

Also on the *23rd of April*, the king and his government evacuated to Crete, while General Papagos resigned and dissolved his general staff, so that there would be no high officers to negotiate with the Germans. (The general was later captured and taken to Germany as a prisoner of war; he was freed by the Americans in 1945.)

The soldiers of the Greek army disbanded and followed whatever road was the shortest route to their homes. Some of the men, however, considered this capitulation the ultimate humiliation. Some even committed suicide instead of surrendering their weapons.

According to the official records, Greek losses amounted to almost eleven thousand men, about eight thousand of whom fell in the Albanian territory. The Italian losses were estimated to be about 11,800. In addition, the Greeks took some 189 officers and 7,645 men as prisoners. After the Greek capitulation to the Germans, the Italians gathered the remains of the Greek and Italian soldiers who had fallen in the areas of Premeti, Klissoura and Height 731 and buried them in shared cemeteries. After the war, the Italian remains were repatriated. Unfortunately, the Greek soldiers' remains were left buried in unmarked graves, except at the cemetery in the village of Vouliarati.

The Germans raised their flag on the Acropolis on the *27th of April*, and on *May 2* Hitler granted freedom to the Greek officers and soldiers who had been considered prisoners of war.

"These three weeks of April, fighting against desperate odds, were for the Greeks the culmination of the hard five months' struggle against Italy in which they expended almost the whole life-strength of their country."[59]

"The Greek campaign had been an old-fashioned gentlemen's war, with honour given and accepted by brave adversaries on each side ..."[60]

---

59 Churchill, Vol. III, p. 207.
60 Keegan, p. 158.

The Greeks, with the British help, fought to defend their home-land from conquest. The Germans battled to overcome them and triumphed, but in a token of respect to the enemy's courage they insisted that the Greek officers should keep their swords. Hitler considered the Greeks the brave descendants of the soldiers of Alexander the Great. "The above acts were the final gestures of chivalry between warriors in a war imminently fated to descend to barbarism."[61] As Churchill said: "We will not say thereafter that the Greeks fight like heroes, but heroes fight like Greeks!"

The quick German victory was due in large part to the superior-ity of the German army and air force. But also, the Greek army was worn to the bone and had no equipment to meet the Germans at the last moment. British aid was inadequate and late. Yugoslavia collapsed, and Turkey remained neutral, but friendly to the Axis.

The Fall of Crete

At the beginning of the Greek-Italian war, the British were respon-sible for the defense of Crete through agreement with the Greek government. The Greek V Division was then sent to fight in the Albanian front.

Hitler, recognizing the importance of Crete in dominating the eastern Mediterranean, issued his directive to occupy Crete on *April 25* (directive #28, code name Mercury). At that time the British had no defensive plan for the island. At the end of April, then, the com-mand of the British and Greek forces was assigned to 2nd New Zea-land Division Major General Freyberg. He, in turn, found that the weapons, ammunition and air defense were completely inadequate; Freyberg requested supplies but only half of those arrived due to ac-tion by the Luftwaffe. The combined British-Greek forces were con-centrated in the Malame, Hania, Rethymno and Iraklio areas. The defensive plan was to protect the island by denying the Germans the use of the airfields and the harbors.

---

61   Keegan, p. 158.

Ultra, the British Intelligence, had decoded the German Enigma machine responsible for most of Luftwaffe communications about the imminent attack. Freyberg wanted to use this intelligence for the defense but General Wavell would not allow him for fear of revealing the source to the Germans. "So important was Ultra that Churchill had decreed that it was better to lose a battle than to lose this source."[62]

The German assault on Crete, "Operation Mercury," started on the *20th of May* and met a determined Anglo-Greek resistance, "Operation Scorcher," which resulted in one of the most brutal and significant conflicts of the war.

The defensive forces in Crete were approximately 11,500 Greeks and 31,500 British, New Zealand and Australian. Superior British naval forces defended the island. The Germans engaged 22,750 men, 1,370 aircraft and 70 ships. They were also supported by a small number of Italian destroyers and torpedo boats.

On the morning of *May 20* the Germans started their air attack in the area of Hania-Maleme with heavy bombardment. Then they began to drop parachutists. Gliders also landed carrying airborne troops. A fierce struggle followed with the 2nd New Zealand Division, which was forced to withdraw further to the southeast. On the same day a paratrooper attack in the Rethymno–Iraklio area resulted in very heavy losses.

On *May 22* a counter attack to recapture Maleme failed. At sea, on the same day, German dive-bombers inflicted huge damage on British ships and crews.[63] The battleships *Warship* and *Valiant* were hit;[64] the cruisers *Gloucester* and *Fiji* sunk. The next day more British boats were destroyed, among them the *Warspite Kelly*, the *Kashmir, Juno, Imperial, Formidable, Perth, Orion, Ajax* and others. When losses were assessed it became clear that the Battle of Crete was the costliest of any British naval engagement in WWII.[65]

---

62 Calvocoressi, Wint and Pritchard, p. 178.
63 Keegan, p. 170.
64 Serving upon the Valiant was Midshipman Prince Philip of Greece. He recorded in his log that fourteen dive-bombers hit the ship (Gilbert, p. 185).
65 Keegan, p. 170.

On the night of *May 23–24* the British-Greek forces moved further southeast, as the Germans advanced. The Germans gained the upper hand and the British began to evacuate. The fighting continued with the islanders' involvement until *May 29*. The majority of the British forces evacuated by midnight on *May 31*. Approximately eighteen thousand troops were successfully rescued in five days from the beaches of Crete, although the Royal Navy suffered heavily. It was a triumph for Hitler's war machinery and a catastrophe for the British-Greek forces.

The British lost one out of every two of their soldiers, and about 11,835 were captured. Of the Greeks, 336 were killed and about fourteen thousand were captured and injured.

Among the elite German paratroopers the casualties exceeded eight thousand men. It was a costly victory for the Germans; it convinced Hitler not to try another such operation. The commander of the XI German Corps, Air Vice Marshall Student, said, "Crete was the tomb of the German Parachutist." Moreover, "... the occupation of Crete would involve the Germans in a bitter anti-partisan campaign, their conduct of which would blacken their name and lay the foundation of a bitter hatred of them not erased in the island to this day."[66]

Churchill considered the attack on Greece a foolish mistake by the Germans. He felt that the Germans wasted their forces in Crete instead of using them in the Middle East.

---

66 Keegan, p. 172.

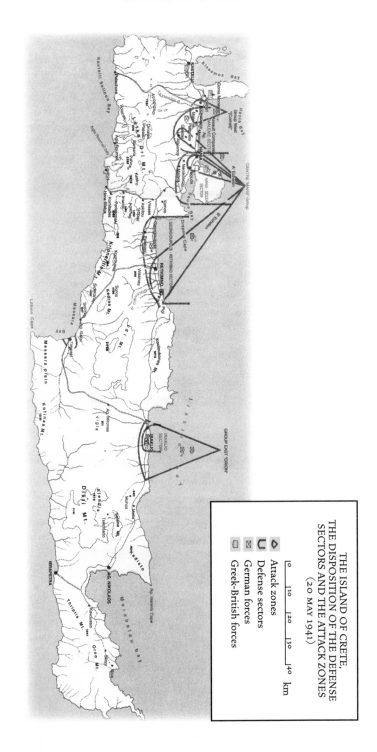

THE ISLAND OF CRETE,
THE DISPOSITION OF THE DEFENSE
SECTORS AND THE ATTACK ZONES
(20 MAY 1941)

Attack zones
Defense sectors
German forces
Greek-British forces

Historical Note: Albania

Albania was the name that the second-century scholar/geographer Ptolemy gave to the lands inhabited by Indo-European tribes named Illyrians in the western Balkans. This land was at the crossroads of Europe and Asia and vulnerable to raids and occupations.

Its fiercely independent people fought against the Romans but were finally occupied around 169 B.C. For six centuries they flourished under the Romans and then under the Eastern Roman, or Byzantine, Empire. As part of the western front of the Byzantine Empire, Huns, Goths, Serbs, Bulgarians and other tribes continuously attacked them. They finally fell to the Turks in 1388 A.D.

The Turkish rule was violent and oppressive. The Turks tried to assimilate the various Albanian tribes through forceful conversion into Islam. Two-thirds of the population converted to Islam.

In 1908 Albanians began to fight the Turks, finally gaining independence in 1912. But Albania's time as an independent nation was brief and turbulent. There was continuous and bloody fighting for dominance among political and tribal factions. As a consequence of the long Ottoman occupation, the country was poor, its people illiterate. Its society was semi-feudal and those in charge corrupt. By 1925 Ahmet Zogu achieved dominance and proclaimed himself king. As King Zog, he tried reforming Albania with a strange combination of Western and Eastern rule. However, without any economic help from the Great Powers and the League of Nations, King Zog's options were limited. He turned instead to Italy, Albania's fascist neighbor, a move that subsequently led to Albania's annexation by Italy in 1939.

The annexation had mixed popularity among Albanians. As the Greek army pushed the Italians into greater Albanian territory they were never certain of the local Albanian allegiances, thus increasing the dangers of war.

Maps and Memorabilia

Honeymoon snapshots.

The newspaper Makedonia, from Thessaloniki, November 23, 1940. The headline reads: "We Have Taken Koritsa."

A map of the front, cut from a newspaper and carried by Dr. Electris with his diaries.

Political cartoons.

Political cartoons.

David and Goliath. Sketch by Paul Polenakis.

After the Battle of Koritsa. Sketch by Paul Polenakis.

A diary sample and letter between Dr. Electris and his wife, Chrysoula.

Θεσ/νίκη τῇ 5 Δεκεμβρίου 1941

ΕΝΤΑΥΘΑ.

Θεωρῶ καθῆκον νά φέρω εἰς γνῶσιν ὑμῶν ὅτι ὁ
Ἰατρός κ.Θεόδωρος Ἠλέκτρης τοῦ Σταύρου, ὑπηρετήσας καθ'
ὅλην τήν διάρκειαν τοῦ πολέμου ἐν τῷ Ἀλβανικῷ Μετώπῳ
εἰς τήν ὑπ'ἐμέ ΧΙην Μεραρχίαν ὡς Ὑγειονομικός Ἀξ/κός
τῆς ΧΙβ Μοίρας Ὀρ.Πυρ/κοῦ, ἐπεδείξατο διαγωγήν ἐξαίρετον
καί ἀντίληψιν τοῦ καθήκοντος ἀξίαν πάσης ἐκτιμήσεως.-

Ἔχω προσωπικήν ἀντίληψιν τῶν κόπων εἰς τούς ὁποίους
ὑπεβλήθη καί τῶν κινδύνων οὕς διέτρεξεν ἐν τῇ ἐκτελέσει
τῆς ὑπηρεσίας του, ὅπως ἐπίσης ἔχω ἀντίληψιν τοῦ ἐνδιαφέ-
ροντός του διά τήν ὑγείαν τῶν μαχητῶν, τῆς λεπτότητος συμπε-
ριφορᾶς καί τῆς καλῆς κοινωνικῆς του ἀνατροφῆς, ὥστε νά
ἁρμόζῃ πᾶς ἔπαινος.-

Συνιστῶ τοῦτον εἰς ὑμᾶς ὅλως ἰδιαιτέρως,θέλων νά
πιστεύω ὅτι διά τῆς τυχόν προσλήψεώς του εἰς τό ὑφ'ὑμᾶς
ἵδρυμα, ὄχι μόνον θά ἀποκτήσητε ἕνα εὐσυνείδητον, συνετόν
καί εὖ ἠγμένον βοηθόν , ἀλλ'ἐν ταυτῷ θ'ἀμοίψητε τάς πρός
τήν Πατρίδα προσφάτους ὑπηρεσίας τοῦ ἐπιστήμονος τούτου
καί διά τάς ὁποίας ἀξίζει προτιμήσεως.-

Μετά πάσης τιμῆς

Σ. Ι. ΔΗΜΑΡΑΤΟΣ
ΕΥΝΙ... ΙΠΠΙΚΟΥ.

Thessaloniki, December 8, 1941

I consider it my duty to inform you that Dr. Theodore Electris, son of Stavros,
served as a medical officer during the whole period of the war at the Albanian
front in the XI B Mountain Artillery Unit, which was under my command. He
displayed exceptional conduct and understanding of his duties that are worth
the highest esteem and regard.

I have personal knowledge of his hard work and high dangers that he underwent
in order to perform his duties as well as his deep interest in the health and
well being of our fighting men as well as his outstanding manners and social
upbringing. He deserves all praise and commendation for his behavior.

I especially recommend him to you. I believe that by employing him in your
Foundation, you will gain a very conscientious assistant, prudent and of
exceptional character, and at the same time you will award this physician
for his latest contributions to our Country for which he deserves preferential
treatment.

Γιά νά θυμούμεθα τό 1940–41.
Ένα δράμα μέ happy end. 7/7/41

"To remember 1940–41, a drama with a happy ending. August 7, 1941."

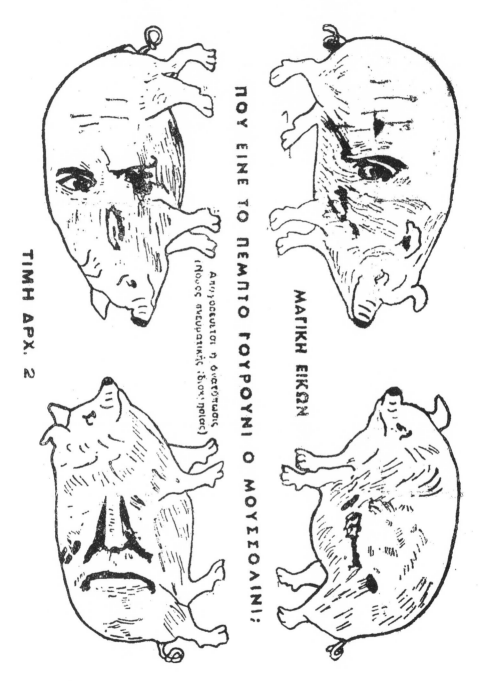

Find the 5th pig.

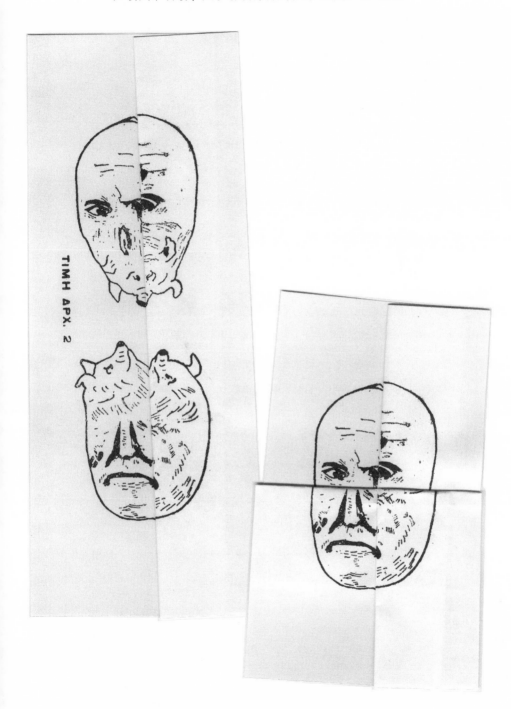

Photocopy the opposite page. Fold as shown to see the face of Mussolini.

Foreword from the Original Edition of
Written on the Knee, Titled *Memoirs from the Front,*
1940–41: A Wartime Journal from the Greek-Italian Front

The Second World War has left its mark on Greece as it has on al-most every other part of Europe, indeed on the rest of the world. Despite the amazing political, economic, social and cultural recon-struction of the post-war world, repercussions from the world con-flict are detectable six decades later. This is especially true of coun-tries like Greece, where invasion and occupation were followed by a ruthless civil war pitting Greek against Greek. Greece, in short, experienced a decade of pitiless war and destruction. The decade of the forties was, in some respects, "the longest night" for the Greeks who began to consider war and famine as a way of life. Deservedly, this period is finally receiving the scholarly attention it merits, and recently some outstanding books have been written on the subject.

Of all the "incidents" of the Second World War in Greece, noth-ing has captured the imagination of the Greeks as much as the so-called Italian invasion of the country and the ensuing Italian-Albanian front, which the Greeks faced during the second year of the war. Most Greeks felt, naively perhaps, that they had done ev-erything possible not to provoke the Axis invasion. This conviction, along with the heroic stand of the Greeks against the Italians and the consequences for Hitler's plans for the invasion of the Balkans and the Soviet Union, account for the prominence of this particu-lar front of the war in the popular and national imagination of the Greeks. Understandably then, this front is the subject of several accounts, literary and historical, published and unpublished. One such account is this remarkable diary by a young reservist doctor. It is the kind of narrative, or eyewitness-to-history account, that re-duces the big schemes of war to something tangible, indeed human. It is the doctor's appropriation of the narrative of the war experi-ence during the approximately six months (October 1940–April

1941), when he served in the mountains of Northern Greece. Such accounts help reduce war to the personal human tragedy that it really is.

I did not have the pleasure of meeting Dr. Theodore Kehribaridies Electris, the author of this diary. But I did have the good fortune of meeting his family approximately a decade after his passing. I first met his widow Chrysoula when she visited Minneapolis on an official visit in the sixties. Soon thereafter, I met the rest of the family, including the daughter Helen Lindsay, editor of both the Greek and English versions of this account, and a person who was destined to make Minneapolis her home base. It was easy to detect from the very beginning of my acquaintance with them that this was a cosmopolitan family with roots reaching beyond Thessaloniki. Because of my interests in Russian history, I was fascinated to have discovered that the father and author of this diary was born in Batum in the Caucusus, that he did part of his studies in Russia, and that the family moved to Greece in the late 1920s. As the editor of this volume cogently puts it, the Second World War "was the fourth in a series of major disruptions that my family endured, following World War I, the Russian Revolution and the Asia Minor Destruction."

Memoirs from the Front, 1940–41 is a remarkable document of observations and impressions by a medical reservist who, like many others, was removed from his comfortable home environment and promising career in Thessaloniki in order to defend his country against an invasion from the North. He reached his thirty-second birthday while serving in the formidable mountains of Northern Greece. It is also the response of a young professional to the impact of war on individuals and society, a response stated in simple direct prose.

The notes in the diary are supplemented by letters to his beloved wife Chrysoula. Many of these letters were sent to Thessaloniki with soldiers whose wounds the doctor had treated and soldiers who were subsequently released.

Through the diary notes and the letters, we learn about the harsh climactic conditions of the mountains of Northern Greece, the rationing of food supplies, medicine and ammunition, the population's reaction to the reality that in addition to feeding themselves and their families they had to help sustain the army, the dynamics between social groups in the army—doctors versus ill-mannered officers, for example—some of the tactical mistakes of Greek officers, the joy that a care package from home brings to soldiers in the front lines, especially when such packages include, as they did at Christmas time, *vasilopites* (special holiday bread), and mundane things such as admiring nature and attempting to capture on film the whole experience at this time in their life. Above all, we learn about the horrors of war, equally catastrophic for invaders and invaded alike—"Dead horses and guns were scattered everywhere." War, after all, does heighten human nature's capacity to behave unseemly, but also provides the opportunity to reflect in the most humane and salutary ways possible. The doctor reminisces about his youth on the Black Sea, about his wife Chrysoula (the golden one) in Thessaloniki who is constantly on his mind. "How can she imagine," he muses, "where we are, where we are wandering and how tangled our lives have become?" These simple lines are reminiscent of the words of a Belgian socialist who a few days after the outbreak of WWI wrote a dedication to a newly written book: "with emotion to the man I used to be."

In his long walks from town to town and from unknown mountain to unknown mountain, the doctor talks to his horse reflectively in order to break the monotony of the daily routine, and in order to make sense out of the madness of war. As he so graphically put it on one occasion when he was climbing the mountains on the way to the village of Fourka, "... for the first time, I saw a dead Italian and my hair stood on end. I thought of his parents, his brothers and sisters, his wife, who were all waiting for him, while he lay thrown on a mountain side in Epirus ... It is possible that we might have the same fate." On another occasion he muses that "Death is never a pretty sight." In the midst of all this madness, the soldiers listen to the wireless field phone for news about the war elsewhere and in a rather unemotional statement he records the news that the Greek army captured Koritsa. The memoir abounds in little details of this sort, details that would delight the professional historian. It is fortunate that the manuscript has been saved from obscurity, and it is hoped that it will have an audience beyond the immediate family circle. Diaries or accounts like *Memoirs from the Front, 1940–41* remind us, among other things, that in the final analysis, all wars are peoples' wars.

THEOFANIS G. STAVROU
PROFESSOR OF HISTORY
DIRECTOR, MODERN GREEK STUDIES
UNIVERSITY OF MINNESOTA

Biographical Notes

The excerpt below is translated from the obituary published in the *Makedonia* newspaper:

"**Theodore Kehribaridies Electris** was born in Batum, Russia, in a thriving and wealthy Greek community. He graduated from the Russian Gymnasium in 1925. Because of the political situation in Russia, after his secondary studies he went to Athens, Greece, as a refugee. There he studied medicine and graduated in 1933. After his military service (10th Infantry Division) he settled in Thessaloniki where he established his practice as an internist. He worked for IKA, the Greek socialized medical system, since the day it was founded. In July of 1940 he married Chrysi Arvanitidou Pappidou. In October of 1940 he was mobilized as a reservist officer of the XI B Artillery Division and served at the front line of the Greek-Italian war in a mountain medical unit as military doctor for the duration of the war. He was honored with a medal for his work.

"After the war the administration of IKA placed him in charge of the large area of Karabournaki, Kalamaria, Aretsou and Votsi. Alone in this whole area, without an assistant, lacking means of transportation for the duration of the German and British occupations of Thessaloniki, he worked superhumanly with faith in his medical science, altruism and self-sacrifice for his patients. He is the doctor who succeeded in founding the medical center for IKA in Kalamaria, which he directed for many years. He was also the doctor for the American Farm School where he worked with equal passion.

"In his district people still remember Phaedia Electris, 'their doctor,' who with such humanity and self-denial came to take care of them at any hour of the day or night."

Dr. Electris and Chrysoula had two children: Pavlos Electris and Eleni (Helen) Electrie Lindsay. They both studied and made their careers in the United States.

The many hardships of the front, as well as his intensive work in occupied and post-World War II Greece, contributed to the untimely death of Dr. Electris on May 31, 1958.

This diary, written at the front during the Greek-Italian war, is dedicated to his beloved wife Chrysoula. It was because of her great love that he overcame all difficulties in order to provide her with every happiness.

Chrysi Pappidou Electrie (Chrysoula) was born in 1917 in Eastern Thrace. Most of the men in her family were wealthy merchants and businessmen who lived and worked around Istanbul and the Black Sea.

After the 1922 exchange of populations, the family reestablished itself in Thessaloniki, Greece. There Chrysoula graduated from Anatolia College and taught English in both Kalamari and Schina Schools.

During the German occupation and the post-WWII years she worked as an assistant to her husband, Dr. Theodore Electris. In 1956 she became the director of the Center of Social Aid (founded by the queen), which was a pioneering institution for Greece at that time. In 1963 she went to the United States as a Fulbright Scholar in order to further her training in social work and psychology.

When the Center of Social Aid became the Center of Mental Health, she continued as its director. Although she lived through some very difficult times—she lost both her husband and her beloved son Pavlos—she lived an exemplary life, productive and dedicated to very high humanistic ideals. She died in February of 1997.

References

The Hellenic Army General Staff. *An Abridged History of the Greek-Italian and Greek-German War 1940–1941: Land Operations*. Athens: Army History Directorate Editions, 1997.

Bauer, Eddy. *Illustrated World War II Encyclopedia*. Tarrytown, NY: Webster's Unified Inc, 1980.

Biberaj, Elez. *Albania: A Socialist Maverick*. Boulder, CO: Westview Press, 1990.

Blau, George E. *Invasion Balkans! The German Campaign in the Balkans: Spring 1941*. Shippensburg, PA: Burd Street Press, 1997.

Calvocoressi, Peter, Guy Wint and John Pritchard. *The Penguin History of the Second World War*. London: Penguin Books, 1999.

Churchill, Winston S. *The Second World War, Vol. 2: Their Finest Hour*. New York: Houghton Mifflin, 1977.

Churchill, Winston S. *The Second World War, Vol. 3: The Grand Alliance*. New York: Houghton Mifflin, 1977.

Dickson, Keith D. *World War II for Dummies*. New York: Hungry Minds, Inc., 2001.

Fowler, Will and Mike Rose. *Their War*. Conshohocken, PA: Combined Publishing, 2000.

Gallant, Thomas W. *Modern Greece*. New York: Oxford University Press, 2001.

Gilbert, Martin. *The Second World War: A Complete History*. New York: Henry Holt Company, Inc., 1989.

Glenny, Misha. *The Balkans: Nationalism, War, and the Great Powers, 1804–1999*. London: Penguin Books, 2000.

Kaliopoulos, John S. and Thanos M. Veremis. *Greece: The Modern Sequel*. London: C. Hurst & Co. (Publishers) Ltd, 2002.

Keegan, John. *The Second World War*. New York: Penguin Books, 1989.

Lukacs, John. *The Last European War: September 1939–December 1941*. New Haven, CT: Yale University Press, 1976.

MacDonald, Callum. *The Lost Battle: Crete 1941*. New York: The Free Press, Macmillan Inc., 1993.

Magenheimer, Heinz. *Hitler's War*. London: Wellington House, 1998.

Mazower, Mark. *Inside Hitler's Greece: The Experience of Occupation, 1941–44*. New Haven, CT: Yale University Press, 1993.

McEvedy, Colin. *The Penguin Atlas Of Recent History*. Middlesex, England: Penguin Press, 1987.

Sakelariou, M.B. *Epirus*. Athens: Ekdotike Athenon S.A., 1997.

Steinhoff, Johanes, Peter Retchel and Dennis Showalter. *Voices From The Third Reich*. New York: Da Capo Press, 1994.

Sulzberger, C. L. *World War II*. Boston: Houghton Mifflin, 1987.

GREEK LANGUAGE SOURCES:

Papagos, A. *Ο ΠΟΛΕΜΟΣ ΤΗΣ ΕΛΛΑΔΟΣ 1940–41 (O Polemos Tis Ellados 1940–41)*. Athens: Goulandri-Horn Foundation.

Richter, Heinz A. *Η ΙΤΑΛΟ-ΓΕΡΜΑΝΙΚΗ ΕΠΙΘΕΣΗ ΕΝΑΝΤΙΟΝ ΤΗΣ ΕΛΛΑΔΟΣ (I Italo-Germaniki Epithesi Enandion Tis Ellados)*. Athens: Govosti Publications, 1998.

Theophanous, Georgios N. *ΧΙΤΛΕΡ ΚΡΗΤΗ ΚΑΙ ΠΕΤΡΕΛΑΙΟ (Hitler Kriti Ke Petreleo: Hitler, Crete and Oil)*. ΙΣΤΟΡΙΑ 411 (Sept. 2002): 78–85.

Image Credits

Army History Directorate of the Hellenic Army General Staff. By Permission #299605, September 14, 2004.

Defense Mapping Agency Aerospace Center. St. Louis, 1993.

Hellenic Literary and Historical Archive (ELIA). 5 Agiou Andreou St, Athens 10556, Hellas.

Historical and Ethnological Society of Greece. Athens.

Museum of War.

2 Rizari St., Athens 10675, Hellas, Greece

Acknowledgements

This book is based on my father's diary, with additional passages added and adapted from letters that he wrote to my mother while he was at the front.

I originally published his diary in Greek without knowing of the existence of all the letters. After settling my mother's estate, I found the letters tied with a red ribbon and carefully preserved in her linen trunk.

I would have left the letters, the diary and all documents in that linen trunk had I not been encouraged by my friend Dru Sweetser to translate them for my children. As she carefully read and edited my translation countless times, she convinced me that the story of my father's six-month expedition is a timeless story of love and war. I would like to thank her for her support.

While I worked on the book, I found that most of my friends in the United States had no knowledge of the Greek involvement and contribution to WWII. Therefore, I felt compelled to present a short historical background, using military maps and historical photographs provided to me by the Hellenic War Museum, the Hellenic Army History Directorate and the Hellenic Library and Historical Archive (ELIA) to make this document come alive. In the context of the overall WWII effort, the profound significance of the Greek story needs to be heard. Although my father's story is but one experience among thousands of Greek soldiers, it bears witness. I view publication of this diary as a tribute to all the crippled veterans who filled the streets of my home city, Thessaloniki, when I was growing up in the 1950s and 60s (including my tutor, who had lost an arm and an eye during the war).

The accurate documentation of my book and my understanding of my father's diary would not have been possible without an excellent book—*An Abridged History Of The Greek-Italian And Greek-German War 1940–1941*—published by the Hellenic Army History

Directorate. I especially have to thank Major-General Dimitrios Gedeon for giving me the book. I also would like to acknowledge the Hellenic Army General Staff for giving me permission to use their maps and photographs, and the dedicated staff of the Hellenic War Museum in Athens for providing me with historically accurate photographs and drawings, as well as the staff of ELIA.

I also wish to thank my husband Dan and his colleague Roger Magnuson for introducing me to a wonderful group of Albanian lawyers and judges— among them Peri Zaharia and Hector Rucio— who enthusiastically provided me with information about events, locations, and names in Albania hitherto unavailable in Greece or the United States.

I am very grateful to Dr. Theofanis Stavrou from the History Department of the University of Minnesota for taking the time to write the foreword and to Sotiris Stavrou for correcting and helping me write my bibliography. I should also thank my editor, Doug Benson, for his assistance and for putting up with all my idiosyncrasies.

Thanks are also due to Nancy Tuminelly and her crew at Mighty Media, including Anders Hanson for the terrific cover and Chris Long for the interior design. At Scarletta Press, I want to thank my editors Alexei Esikoff and especially Ian Graham Leask, who from the start was convinced my little book deserved a second life and who had the vision to match the subject matter with the interests of the fascinating novelist, Louis de Bernières. Thanks, Louis, for your kind introduction.

Last, but far from least, I would like to thank my son Alexander Lindsay, who diligently organized and digitized all the photographs and created some of the maps and artwork for the front and back cover and encouraged me to "JUST DO IT."

Color Addendum

Included among Dr. Electris' belongings are a medical military guide to chemical warfare, the diary, photographs, a small acorn inscribed with the date it was found (November 21, 1941), flowers Chrysoula kept and letters they had written to each other.

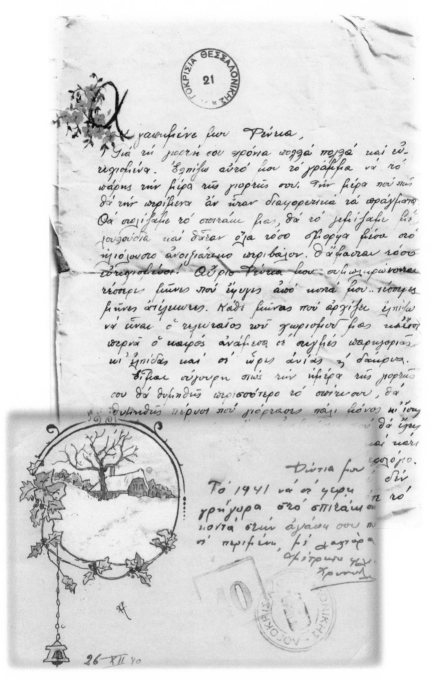

Chrysoula wrote this letter to Dr. Electris in honor of his name day (March 8). In the foreground is her hand-drawn Christmas card.

Permit for entrance into Germany.

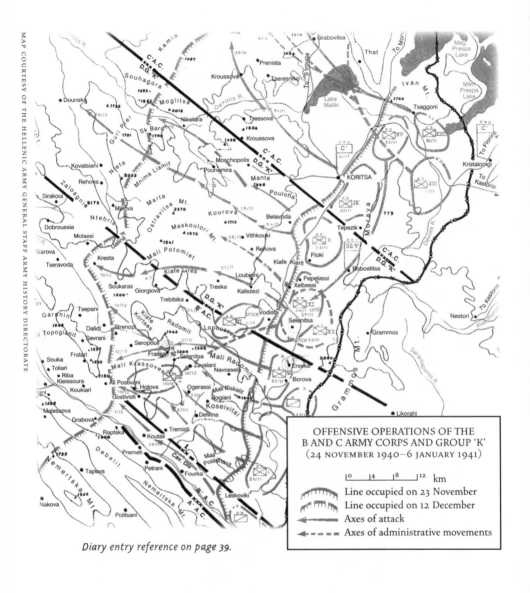

OFFENSIVE OPERATIONS OF THE
B AND C ARMY CORPS AND GROUP 'K'
(24 NOVEMBER 1940–6 JANUARY 1941)

| 0 | 4 | 8 | 12 | km |

Line occupied on 23 November
Line occupied on 12 December
Axes of attack
Axes of administrative movements

Diary entry reference on page 39.

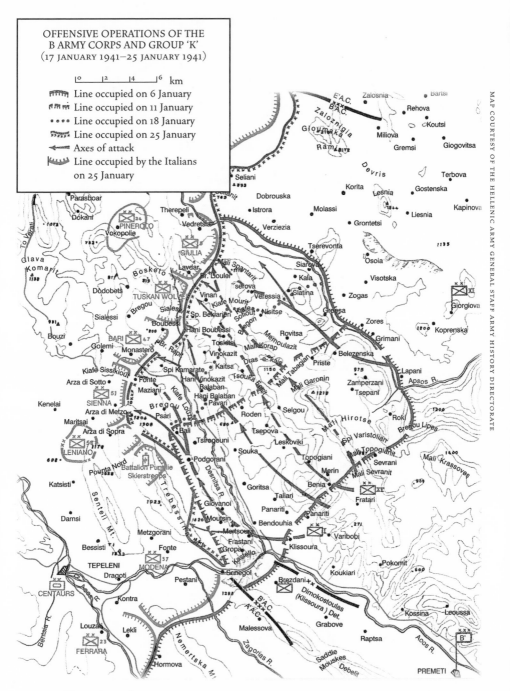

OFFENSIVE OPERATIONS OF THE
B ARMY CORPS AND GROUP 'K'
(17 JANUARY 1941–25 JANUARY 1941)

0   2   4   6 km

〰〰 Line occupied on 6 January
〰〰 Line occupied on 11 January
•••• Line occupied on 18 January
〰〰 Line occupied on 25 January
◄— Axes of attack
〰〰 Line occupied by the Italians
     on 25 January

Diary entry reference on page 53.

ITALIAN "PRIMAVERA" (SPRING) ATTACK
(9 MARCH 1941–15 MARCH 1941)

0   1   2   3 km

Line occupied by Greek forces
Line occupied by Italian forces
Italian directions of attack
Line occupied by the Italians
after the attack

Istore

Therepeli

22
ALPINE CHASSEURS

Apsos R.

Bozout

Spathara

BLACK SHIRT

Lavdari

931

Bosketto

819

Dodovetsi

59 717
KAGLIARI

869

Bregou Loulei

Mali Spadarit
1110

850

xx+
+I 960

961

Boubessi Saddle

Kiafe Mourit

XI

802

Sialessi

1231

Nitsista

800

Kiafe Sofiout

757

Hani Boubessi

Bregou Memoulazit
1242

1014

678

Boubessi

710

Toskitsi

Mali Korap

Golemi

38
PUGLIE

705

Monastero

717

Bregou

XV
xx
I

Rapit

XV
xx
I

XV
Kaitsa 1123

Dras - e - Ka

Golemi

731

BLACK
SHIRT

Fonde

Hani
Vinokazit

Mali Tabayia

Tsouka Fessik

Arza di Sotto

-1030

Balaban

24
PINEROLO

-1060

Hani
Balaban

Pavari

XX
I

Maziani

Ronten

Selg

Arza di Mezzo

679

I 1308

xx
V

I
xx
V

Psari

736

630

Maritsai

1425

Arza di Sopra

Mpali

Desnitsa R.

Trebessina

Tserogouni

Proi Tsepova R.

1710

Souka

1816

xx
V

Athenas Metzgoranis

Podgorani

Goritsa

Diary entry reference on page 118.

THE BALKAN CAMPAIGN
DISPOSITION AND OPERATION PLAN
OF THE 12th GERMAN ARMY

| 0 | 50 | 100 | 150 | 200 | km |

+———+ Railway line
⊓⊓⊓⊓⊓⊓ "Metaxas" defensive line
⌒⌒⌒ Vermio defensive area
▬▬▬ Northern Epirus front
→ Axes of advance of the Germans

Diary entry reference on page 192.

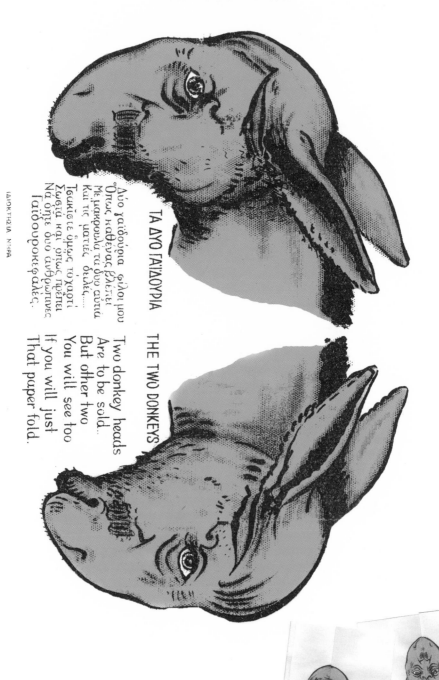

ΙΔΙΟΚΤΗΣΙΑ Ν44ΡΑ

ΤΑ ΔΥΟ ΓΑΪΔΟΥΡΙΑ

Δύο γαϊδούρια φίλοι μου
Όπως καθένας βλέπει
Με μακρουλά τα δυο αυτιά
Καί τις ματιές δειλές...
Τσακίστε όμως τόχαρτί
Ζωγιά καί όπως πρέπει
Νά δήτε δυο ανθρώπινες
Γαϊδουροκεφαλές.

THE TWO DONKEYS

Two donkey heads
Are to be sold...
But other two
You will see too
If you will just
That paper fold.

Photocopy this page and fold as shown
to see two evil men: Hitler and Mussolini.